THE SON

by Florian Zeller

translated by Christopher Hampton

∥SAMUEL FRENCH∥

Copyright © 2021 by Florian Zeller
All Rights Reserved

THE SON is fully protected under the copyright laws of the British Commonwealth, including Canada, the United States of America, and all other countries of the Copyright Union. All rights, including professional and amateur stage productions, recitation, lecturing, public reading, motion picture, radio broadcasting, television, online/digital production, and the rights of translation into foreign languages are strictly reserved.

ISBN 978-0-573-13276-6

concordtheatricals.co.uk
concordtheatricals.com

FOR AMATEUR PRODUCTION ENQUIRIES

United Kingdom and World
excluding North America
licensing@concordtheatricals.co.uk
020-7054-7200

Each title is subject to availability from Concord Theatricals, depending upon country of performance.

CAUTION: Professional and amateur producers are hereby warned that *THE SON* is subject to a licensing fee. The purchase, renting, lending or use of this book does not constitute a license to perform this title(s), which license must be obtained from the appropriate agent prior to any performance. Performance of this title(s) without a license is a violation of copyright law and may subject the producer and/or presenter of such performances to penalties. Both amateurs and professionals considering a production are strongly advised to apply to the appropriate agent before starting rehearsals, advertising, or booking a theatre. A licensing fee must be paid whether the title is presented for charity or gain and whether or not admission is charged.

This work is published by Samuel French, an imprint of Concord Theatricals. Ltd

All professional performance rights whatsoever in these plays are strictly reserved and application for professional performance in the English language etc should be made to the Translator's agent, Casarotto Ramsay and Associates Limited, 3rd Floor, 7 Savoy Court, Strand, London, WC2R 0EX(tel: 020 7287 4450, email: rights@casarotto.co.uk) acting on behalf of the original author's agent.

Application for performance in any language except English, should be made to the Author's agent, Drama Literary Agency, 24 rue Feydeau,

Paris 75002, France. www.dramaparis.com. No performance may be given unless a licence has been obtained.

No one shall make any changes in this title for the purpose of production. No part of this book may be reproduced, stored in a retrieval system, scanned, uploaded, or transmitted in any form, by any means, now known or yet to be invented, including mechanical, electronic, digital, photocopying, recording, videotaping, or otherwise, without the prior written permission of the publisher. No one shall share this title, or part of this title, to any social media or file hosting websites.

The moral right of Florian Zeller and Christopher Hampton to be identified as author of this work has been asserted in accordance with Section 77 of the Copyright, Designs and Patents Act 1988.

USE OF COPYRIGHTED MUSIC

A licence issued by Concord Theatricals to perform this play does not include permission to use the incidental music specified in this publication. In the United Kingdom: Where the place of performance is already licensed by the PERFORMING RIGHT SOCIETY (PRS) a return of the music used must be made to them. If the place of performance is not so licensed then application should be made to PRS for Music (www.prsformusic.com). A separate and additional licence from PHONOGRAPHIC PERFORMANCE LTD (www. ppluk.com) may be needed whenever commercial recordings are used. Outside the United Kingdom: Please contact the appropriate music licensing authority in your territory for the rights to any incidental music.

USE OF COPYRIGHTED THIRD-PARTY MATERIALS

Licensees are solely responsible for obtaining formal written permission from copyright owners to use copyrighted third-party materials (e.g., artworks, logos) in the performance of this play and are strongly cautioned to do so. If no such permission is obtained by the licensee, then the licensee must use only original materials that the licensee owns and controls. Licensees are solely responsible and liable for clearances of all third-party copyrighted materials, and shall indemnify the copyright owners of the play(s) and their licensing agent, Concord Theatricals Ltd., against any costs, expenses, losses and liabilities arising from the use of such copyrighted third-party materials by licensees.

IMPORTANT BILLING AND CREDIT REQUIREMENTS

If you have obtained performance rights to this title, please refer to your licensing agreement for important billing and credit requirements.

THE SON in this translation by Christopher Hampton was first presented at the Kiln Theatre, London, on 20 February 2019. Directed by Michael Longhurst, Designer Lizzie Clachan, Lighting Designer Lee Curran, Composer and Sound Designer Isobel Waller-Bridge, Casting Director Amy Ball, Assistant Director Atri Banerjee. The cast was as follows:

ANNE . . . . Amanda Abbington
NICOLAS . . . . Laurie Kynaston
PIERRE . . . . John Light
SOFIA . . . . Amaka Okafor
NURSE . . . . Oseloka Obi
DOCTOR . . . . Martin Turner

This production transferred to the Duke of York's Theatre, London, on 24 August 2019, with Cudjoe Asare taking over the role of the Nurse. The Associate Director was Tom Hughes and Associate Lighting Designer Charlotte Burton.

Le Fils in its original French production opened at the Comédie des Champs-Elysées, Paris, in February 2018, directed by Ladislas Chollat, with Stéphane Freiss, Rod Paradot, Florence Darel, Élodie Navarre, Raphael Magnabosco and Daniel San Pedro.

CHARACTERS

PIERRE
ANNE
SOFIA
NICOLAS
NURSE
DOCTOR

SETTING

Pierre's flat, Anne's flat and a waiting-room and doctor's office in a hospital, all in Paris.

TIME

Present.

ONE

(**PIERRE**'s *flat*. **ANNE** *stands facing him. He looks tense.*)

PIERRE. What are you doing here?

(**ANNE** *doesn't answer.*)

Anne, I'm speaking to you…

ANNE. I …

PIERRE. Yes?

ANNE. I don't know, I …

PIERRE. You don't know?

ANNE. No, sorry. I mean, I don't know where to begin. I …

PIERRE. Has something happened?

(**PIERRE** *is looking behind her, as if he's afraid that at any moment, someone might come out of the bedroom.*)

You turn up with no warning… You know very well…

ANNE. I tried to call, but you weren't answering.

PIERRE. Why? Is there a problem?

ANNE. Is she here?

PIERRE. Mm?

ANNE. Is she here?

PIERRE. She's putting the baby to bed. Why?

ANNE. I didn't want to disturb you. But you never pick up. And I had to speak to you. One way or another.

PIERRE. What's the matter?

ANNE. It's Nicolas.

PIERRE. Oh, yes? Has something happened?

ANNE. Yes. He's not well. And I'm not well either. It's too difficult. I can't manage it.

PIERRE. You can't manage what?

ANNE. It's just impossible. I... I don't know what to do any more. I... this morning, I was summoned to the school, and the headmaster...

> (**PIERRE** *exhales. She stops dead in the middle of her sentence.* **PIERRE** *notices.*)

PIERRE. What?

ANNE. Am I disturbing you? You're making a face, as if I'm disturbing you.

PIERRE. Of course not.

ANNE. It's your son I'm talking about!

PIERRE. I know.

ANNE. You ought to be just a little bit concerned...

PIERRE. Obviously I'm concerned! Why are you saying these things?

ANNE. Because you've got this expression. As if I was here to annoy you with problems about... with my problems. When I'm talking to you about Nicolas!

PIERRE. I'm sorry. I'm just a bit... tired. You know what it is, the baby's still not sleeping through and...

ANNE. *(Interrupting him.)* Anyway, he summoned me. The headmaster. To find out what was going on. And that's when I found out he hadn't been to school for more than three months…

PIERRE. What?

ANNE. I'm telling you. For three months he's been pretending… every morning.

PIERRE. What are you talking about?

ANNE. I'm explaining the situation to you and I …

PIERRE. Wait a minute… he hasn't been to school for three months? And during all this time, you never noticed anything?

ANNE. No.

PIERRE. How is that possible?

ANNE. He set off every morning with his bag and everything he needed for the day, but he didn't go there.

PIERRE. Are you joking? What was he doing? I mean, all day… for three months! Where did he go?

ANNE. I don't know. He hardly ever answers when I ask him a question. He behaves as if I don't exist.

PIERRE. But why?

ANNE. I don't know. I'm worried about him, Pierre. He's not like he was before. Believe me. I don't know what's happened, but something has. He's changed. He… and I'm wondering if… to be absolutely honest with you… I'm even wondering if…

PIERRE. If what?

>   (**SOFIA** *comes in. Tense moment.* **PIERRE** *tries to justify* **ANNE***'s presence.*)

Ah, Sofia, I …

SOFIA. *(Hostile.)* What's going on?

PIERRE. Anne has come to talk to me about Nicolas. It's just been discovered he hasn't been going to school, and...

ANNE. It's not just that, Pierre... he's not well.

PIERRE. Yes, he's not well at the moment, and...

ANNE. He hasn't been well for months.

SOFIA. Ever since Pierre left you, I expect...

PIERRE. Sofia, please.

(Pause.)

And the headmaster? What did he say?

ANNE. They want to expel him.

PIERRE. Unbelievable! Have you told Nicolas?

ANNE. Yes. But he couldn't care less...

PIERRE. What's going on in his head?

ANNE. You have to speak to him, Pierre. I can't manage it anymore. He needs you. You can't abandon him.

PIERRE. I'm not abandoning him! Why are you saying that?

ANNE. The other day, I simply asked him to – I can't even remember what, something trivial, to clear his plate away or something like that – and he looked at me with such... with such hatred. I thought he was going to...

PIERRE. To what?

ANNE. He frightens me, do you understand?

(Pause.)

PIERRE. I'll go and see him tomorrow. All right? I'll drop in at the end of the day. Will he be there?

ANNE. Yes.

PIERRE. I'll drop in and see him. Don't worry.

ANNE. Thanks.

> (**ANNE** *makes an affectionate gesture to thank him. It's not even as much as a gesture, just a hint, a sketch, but it's enough to make* **PIERRE** *feel embarrassed in front of* **SOFIA**.)

He was such a sweet child. So wonderful. Do you remember? So sensitive. I don't know what's happened…

> (*In the distance, the baby starts crying.* **SOFIA** *hesitates, then leaves the room.*)

PIERRE. Come on. Don't worry. Everything'll go back to normal.

ANNE. You think so?

PIERRE. Of course.

ANNE. I don't know.

PIERRE. Yes, it will. Don't worry. I'm here.

ANNE. No, that's exactly it. You're not here any more.

> (*Pause. Blackout.*)

TWO

(A different room. **NICOLAS** *is sitting on the sofa. He's biting his nails.* **PIERRE** *is standing in front of him.)*

PIERRE. I wanted to talk to you, Nicolas… that's… that's why I've come home. You know, I mean… here.

(Pause.)

Are you listening to me?

NICOLAS. Yes.

PIERRE. I know you're having a difficult time and things aren't easy for you… I also know you're angry with me… but we have to talk. Both of us.

*(***PIERRE** *sits down. Pause.)*

Your mother told me that you haven't been going to school.

*(***NICOLAS** *shrugs his shoulders.)*

What's going on?

NICOLAS. Nothing.

PIERRE. Don't say "nothing". Explain it to me.

(Pause.)

Nicolas? Why have you stopped going to school?

NICOLAS. I don't know.

PIERRE. You don't know?

NICOLAS. No.

PIERRE. There must be a reason?

    (**NICOLAS** *shrugs his shoulders.*)

You can't decide to stop going to school, just like that. It's not an option. Do you hear what I'm saying?

NICOLAS. Yes.

    (*Pause.*)

PIERRE. Are you having problems?

    (**NICOLAS** *sighs.*)

What? Why are you sighing?

NICOLAS. No reason.

PIERRE. Nicolas, I can't help you if you won't tell me anything. And stop biting your nails like that!

    (*Pause.*)

I've spoken to your mother. She tells me you don't sleep at night. That you pace up and down in your room… that you… what is it you're up to?

NICOLAS. Nothing.

    (*Pause.*)

PIERRE. And school… I mean… what are you going to do? Are you going to repeat a year? Is that your plan?

NICOLAS. I really couldn't give a shit.

PIERRE. Terrific! Great attitude…

    (*Pause.*)

What were you doing? All those days… where did you go?

NICOLAS. I walked.

PIERRE. You walked?

NICOLAS. Yes.

PIERRE. On your own?

NICOLAS. Yes.

PIERRE. You walked on your own in the street?

NICOLAS. Or in the park.

PIERRE. But why?

(NICOLAS *shrugs his shoulders.*)

Come on, Nicolas! Do you understand what's going on? Do you honestly believe that this is acceptable? Because you needed to stretch your legs? And in your exam year, as well... doesn't make any sense!

(*Pause.*)

It didn't occur to you that eventually your school would get in touch with us?

NICOLAS. I wasn't feeling well. Walking was the only thing that relaxed me.

PIERRE. Why weren't you feeling well?

(*He doesn't answer.*)

All right, let's say you weren't feeling well! But that's no reason to just give up... in life, you have to struggle.

NICOLAS. I don't want to struggle any more.

PIERRE. But why? What's the matter with you?

(*Pause.*)

Nicolas... talk to me.

(*Pause.* NICOLAS *starts biting his nails again.*)

I don't understand. A couple of years ago, you always had this big smile on your face. And then all of a sudden... what happened to you?

(Pause.)

Your mother's at the end of her tether, you know that? She tells me you're making her life a living hell. That you haven't been behaving well towards her. Is that true?

(Pause.)

She wants to send you to boarding school. Did you know that? Is that what you want?

NICOLAS. No.

PIERRE. So?

*(**NICOLAS** shrugs his shoulders. All the same, it's clear that the mention of boarding school has unsettled him.)*

You have to do something, Nicolas. You can't just let things go like this...

NICOLAS. I can't manage it.

PIERRE. What makes you say that?

(Pause.)

(More gently.) Has something happened at school? I mean...

NICOLAS. No.

PIERRE. Or outside of school?... We can talk to one another, you know.

NICOLAS. It's not that. It's...

PIERRE. Yes?

NICOLAS. I don't know how to describe it.

PIERRE. Tell me in your own words.

NICOLAS. *(Sincerely.)* It's life, it's weighing me down.

> *(Brief pause.* **PIERRE** *seems moved by this unexpected confidence.)*

PIERRE. But why? What is it about your life that isn't working?

NICOLAS. I don't know.

> *(Pause.)*

I've been telling myself that... maybe...

PIERRE. Go on.

NICOLAS. No. Nothing. Forget it.

PIERRE. No, tell me...

> *(***NICOLAS*** is hesitating.)*

Nicolas, tell me.

NICOLAS. I'd like to live with you.

PIERRE. *(Caught offguard.)* You... you mean...

NICOLAS. I can't go on here. Because I know I could get out of this. But not here. Not on my own. It's too difficult...

PIERRE. Yes, but...

NICOLAS. Me and Mum aren't getting on. She can't put up with me any more... She's at the end of her tether, I know she is. And when I'm here, I get too many black ideas. It's too difficult. I promise you. And I know it's just going to get worse and worse. I feel it. Also, I'd like to live with my little brother...

PIERRE. *(Embarrassed.)* Yes.

NICOLAS. If you send me to boarding school, I'll go crazy.

PIERRE. Of course you won't.

NICOLAS. Yes, I will, I promise you. My head feels like it's exploding.

PIERRE. Come on, come here.

> *(***PIERRE** *takes him in his arms.)*

NICOLAS. Sometimes I feel as if I am going crazy, Dad.

> *(***PIERRE** *hugs him closer.)*

PIERRE. What are you talking about?

NICOLAS. I'm telling you. I don't understand what's happening to me.

PIERRE. Come on...

NICOLAS. I don't understand.

> *(***NICOLAS** *weeps.* **PIERRE** *is unsettled.)*

PIERRE. Don't worry. We'll get out of this. Mm? Don't worry. We'll find a solution. Come on... trust me.

> *(He comforts him.* **NICOLAS** *is like a small child. Blackout.)*

THREE

(**PIERRE**'s *flat. Tense silence between* **SOFIA** *and* **PIERRE**. *It stretches out.*)

PIERRE. Why are you taking it like this?

SOFIA. Taking it like what?

(*Pause.*)

PIERRE. I can't just abandon him.

SOFIA. Why are you talking about abandoning him? She's just telling you these things to make you feel guilty.

PIERRE. That's got nothing to do with it, Sofia. Please… He's going through a difficult phase. That's a fact.

(*Pause.*)

He can stay in my office. I'll put a bed in there. Just temporary.

SOFIA. And what about school?

PIERRE. We'll work something out. There must be a school which would take him in mid-year. Don't you think?

SOFIA. I'm sure.

PIERRE. You've only known him for two years and I can see that… I mean, I know you have a negative impression of him… after everything that happened… but he hasn't always been like this. When he was younger… he was so…

(*Pause.*)

There were marks on his forearm.

SOFIA. What?

PIERRE. When I went to see him just now, I saw he had, I don't know, marks.

SOFIA. What kind of marks?

PIERRE. Little scars all up his arm... as if he'd... well, you know what I mean... it upset me so much. My little boy... I'd do anything for him, anything. And today, there he was, in front of me, suffering... and what am I doing for him? I mean, you only do that kind of thing when you're suffering, right?

(**SOFIA** *makes an affectionate gesture.*)

SOFIA. Come on...

PIERRE. And it's true, you're right, I'm feeling guilty. I know it started when... I can't pretend I'm not responsible for the situation. I left, Sofia.

SOFIA. I don't see the connection.

(**PIERRE** *shrugs his shoulders.*)

It's not your fault if he isn't well.

PIERRE. I don't know.

SOFIA. It's nothing to do with...

(*She prefers not to complete the sentence.*)

It's nothing to do with it, Pierre!

PIERRE. You know, I made him cry. When I told him I was leaving his mother, I made him cry. It's not an image I can easily forget.

SOFIA. I understand. But you're not the first man to... this has nothing to do with what's going on today. Believe me. It's a difficult time for him. Simple as that.

PIERRE. Anyway, there's nothing else I can do. I can't just give up on him.

SOFIA. I understand. Don't worry.

(*He smiles at her, as if to thank her.*)

PIERRE. When I was his age, my mother was already ill. I was thinking about it just now... I... I went to see her every day in hospital and sat with her. I revised for my exams on a little table opposite her, while she... while she was dying... It was horribly sad. My father never showed up. Too busy living his life. He had his business... his famous hunting parties... he travelled all the time. But a week before... before she died... I ran into someone on the street, a family friend, who told me he'd had dinner with him the night before... I didn't even know he was in Paris... and he hadn't thought it was worth telling us, or coming in to see her...

SOFIA. Why are you telling me this?

PIERRE. I don't know. Sorry. No reason. I ... It's all mixed up in my head. What I wanted to say is that I don't want to be that kind of man. That kind of father.

(*Pause.*)

SOFIA. What about us?

PIERRE. What?

SOFIA. What about us? Our life?... Sacha.

PIERRE. It won't make any difference to Sacha. We'll look after him exactly the same way.

SOFIA. You think so?

PIERRE. Of course... trust me. It's not going to change anything in our lives. I promise you.

(*She smiles. She'd like to believe it.*)

Everything'll be fine. You'll see, darling. Everything'll be fine.

(But, like a mental image, **NICOLAS** *comes slowly into the room. He approaches a chest of drawers or a cupboard, then, with a violent gesture, tips all its contents on to the floor, as well as everything he sees in front of him – as if he wanted to wreck the place completely.* **SOFIA** *stands, appalled, in front of her destroyed flat. As for* **PIERRE**, *he doesn't seem to notice. Blackout.)*

FOUR

(The flat. The things are still all over the floor, books, a lamp, a piece of furniture, etc. But everyone behaves as if everything is normal. Morning. **NICOLAS** *is sitting on the sofa. He's staring into space. Suddenly,* **PIERRE** *comes in. He starts, seeing* **NICOLAS**.*)*

PIERRE. Ah, you're here! Did you sleep well?

(He kisses **NICOLAS**'s *hair.)*

And there's your mother telling me you never get up before noon...

(Pause.)

All right? I didn't expect you to be up so early...

NICOLAS. I woke up and then I couldn't get back to sleep.

PIERRE. Always takes a bit of time getting used to a new place, haven't you noticed?

*(**NICOLAS** shrugs his shoulders.)*

Sacha didn't wake you, did he?

NICOLAS. No.

PIERRE. He cried a lot last night... you didn't hear him?

NICOLAS. No.

PIERRE. Good.

(He makes himself a coffee.)

You want anything? A coffee?

*(**NICOLAS** shakes his head.)*

You don't have anything in the morning?

NICOLAS. Why was he crying?

PIERRE. Your brother? He doesn't sleep through yet. He was hungry, that's all.

*(Pause. **NICOLAS** bites his nails. **PIERRE** notices.)*

You were the same, you weren't a great sleeper. I mean, when you were a baby...

*(**PIERRE** notices that **NICOLAS** is elsewhere.)*

Are you listening to me?

NICOLAS. Mm?

PIERRE. What's the matter?

NICOLAS. No, it's just... I was thinking about... about the set-up. And I... I mean, I'm not sure...

PIERRE. What?

*(**NICOLAS** seems reluctant to answer.)*

What are you not sure about?

NICOLAS. I'm feeling a bit uncomfortable here... I feel I'm disturbing you both...

PIERRE. Of course not! What makes you say that?

NICOLAS. And Sofia... I don't think she likes me. Did she really agree to my moving in here?

PIERRE. Obviously, Nicolas. Obviously.

(Pause.)

NICOLAS. But it's not only that. There's this school as well... I don't know if I feel right about going there.

PIERRE. Sorry?

NICOLAS. I've been thinking about it this morning. Everyone's going to wonder why I'm showing up like this in the middle of a year...

PIERRE. So?

NICOLAS. I won't know what to say to them.

PIERRE. You can say anything you like... Why are you worrying so much about what other people think?

NICOLAS. They're bound to look at me strangely...

PIERRE. No, they won't... on the contrary... someone who arrives in the middle of a year, they'll be interested in you, curious... wonder where you come from.

NICOLAS. Exactly. I don't want to answer a lot of questions. I don't want to have to tell them what's been going on.

PIERRE. Listen, Nicolas... you're not the first person to change schools in the middle of a year... it happens all the time. I understand it might make you a bit anxious, but that's the way things are. All you have to do is not get thrown out.

NICOLAS. I know, but I was thinking... I've missed so many lessons this year... because of being absent so often... I'm full of gaps... I'll never be ready in time to take the exams. And it's April already... it's almost the end of the school year... I'm stressed about it, you know? And I was wondering if it might be better to start again in September with less pressure and –

PIERRE. *(Interrupting him.)* You'll go back on Monday, Nicolas. It's not negotiable. We've already discussed this.

(Pause.)

Why are you worrying like this? It'll be fine.

NICOLAS. I don't know.

PIERRE. You asked me if you could come and live here. I agreed, and that's fine, but it won't work unless you make an effort. Understand? We can't go on like this indefinitely... going round in circles. Hanging about. Things have to change. And stop biting your nails, you're going to make them bleed!

> *(Pause.* **PIERRE** *pulls himself together. He comes and sits next to* **NICOLAS**.*)*

(More gently.) You've been depressed. It can happen to anyone. That they end up on their knees... understand what I'm saying? To anyone. And now, it's time to stand up again.

NICOLAS. Yes.

PIERRE. I want this to be a new start. I want to see you smile again... the way you used to smile.

> *(Pause.)*

You're an extraordinary boy. With a bit of work, you'll have no difficulty catching up... I have confidence in you. I'm sure one day you'll look back on this whole period... and you'll say...

> *(***PIERRE*** appears to hesitate.)*

NICOLAS. What?

PIERRE. You'll even have forgotten the reasons you weren't well.

NICOLAS. I don't know.

PIERRE. You will! Trust me... we've all been through this. We've all had difficult moments. You just have to accept it.

NICOLAS. Other people don't feel like this. For them, everything's easy.

PIERRE. How do you know?

NICOLAS. I watch them... all they think about is having a laugh, having fun.

PIERRE. You're not in their head. Believe me, everybody has problems and fears and... you just have to get past them. That's why you're going back to school, starting Monday. Do you understand?

>   *(Pause.)*

Nicolas, do you understand?

NICOLAS. Yes.

>   (**NICOLAS** *stands up. He looks upset. He heads towards his room.*)

PIERRE. You don't want anything for breakfast?

NICOLAS. No.

PIERRE. Where are you going?

NICOLAS. Back to bed.

>   (**PIERRE** *sighs.* **NICOLAS** *heads for his room. Just before he leaves, he turns back to his father. Brief pause.*)

Dad?

PIERRE. Yes?

NICOLAS. Thanks for everything you're doing for me.

>   (**PIERRE** *is surprised by the sincerity of this remark. He smiles at him.* **NICOLAS** *has a go at a smile. He goes out. Blackout.*)

FIVE

(**PIERRE**'s *flat. Morning. The things are still all over the floor and, in the same way, everyone behaves as if this chaos didn't exist.* **SOFIA** *is preparing breakfast. She moves towards the door to* **NICOLAS**'s *room.*)

SOFIA. Nicolas? Are you ready? It's time to go.

(*A buzzer goes off in the kitchen. She hurries to deal with it.*)

(*On her way.*) Nicolas? Do you hear me?

(*She disappears into the kitchen for a minute.*)

(*Offstage.*) I've made your coffee. You just about have time to drink it.

(*She comes back into the room.*)

Nicolas?

(*She crosses the room and knocks on* **NICOLAS**'s *door.*)

Nicolas? You're going to be late.

(*Pause.*)

Nicolas, I must have called you at least ten times. We can't do this every morning... do you hear me?

(*Pause.*)

Nicolas, I'm speaking to you! Open the door...

(Pause.)

It's time. You can't be late every day... you were yesterday... do you hear me?

(The door suddenly opens.)

Why don't you answer me?

NICOLAS. I do answer you.

SOFIA. It's time. You have to go.

NICOLAS. I know.

SOFIA. Come on. I made you a coffee. Sit down. You have just enough time.

*(**SOFIA** goes into the kitchen to fetch the coffee. **NICOLAS** sits down.)*

(Offstage.) I have to prepare your little brother's bottle as well. I'd better not keep him waiting. I'll hear about it if I do.

*(**NICOLAS** buries his face in his hands.)*

NICOLAS. Where's my father?

SOFIA. *(Offstage.)* He's already left. He had a very early meeting this morning.

(She comes back with a coffee.)

Here's your coffee. Do you want anything else?

*(**SOFIA** notices **NICOLAS** has his head in his hands.)*

What's the matter?

*(He doesn't answer. **SOFIA** goes to him.)*

Nicolas? What's the matter with you?

NICOLAS. Nothing.

SOFIA. Is... are you in pain?

(He doesn't answer. You might think he was crying, but you can't see his face.)

Nicolas, what's going on? Tell me.

NICOLAS. I don't know.

SOFIA. Are you unhappy?

(He doesn't deny it.)

Why are you unhappy?

NICOLAS. I don't know.

SOFIA. You don't know?

NICOLAS. No.

SOFIA. Do you often start crying like this for no reason?

(He doesn't answer.)

Nicolas? Does this often happen?

NICOLAS. I'm not crying.

*(Brief pause. **SOFIA** is confused. She doesn't know what to do.)*

SOFIA. What's the matter?

NICOLAS. I can't seem to understand the point of it!

SOFIA. Of what?

NICOLAS. Anything... Life...

SOFIA. The point of life?

(She seems confused.)

Sometimes, you have to decide not to ask yourself that question. Don't you think? You have to be content with moving forward... and not brood about things too much.

(She puts an arm around his shoulders, as if to console him.)

You're all right here, aren't you? In your new room? You wanted to live here. And see, we organised everything to make it possible. That ought to make you feel better... doesn't it? Look how fond your father is of you. He never stops talking about you. Mm? Come on... you have to be brave.

NICOLAS. Yes.

SOFIA. And there's your brother as well... he's only little now, but soon you'll be able to teach him stuff and play with him... mm? You're important to him. Come on...

NICOLAS. Yes. Sorry. I'm really sorry. I don't know what came over me.

SOFIA. Don't apologise, it can happen to anyone...

*(**NICOLAS** dries his tears and takes his coffee.)*

Better?

NICOLAS. Yes. Thanks.

SOFIA. Come on...

NICOLAS. Yes. I have to go.

(He stands and picks up his bag.)

Can I ask you a question?

SOFIA. Of course.

NICOLAS. When you met my father... Did you know he was married?

SOFIA. Mm? I ...

NICOLAS. Did you?

SOFIA. Yes.

(Pause.)

But he told me straight away that...

NICOLAS. That what?

SOFIA. Perhaps it's better if you talk to him about this, don't you think?

NICOLAS. I don't know.

SOFIA. I think it'd be better. Especially as it's time to go now...

NICOLAS. You know, when he left, my mother took it so badly... she really suffered. And she never stopped saying awful things about him... whereas I worshipped him. I mean... it was as if I'd been chopped in half. And from then on, I didn't know what to think any more.

SOFIA. I understand. It's not an easy situation...

NICOLAS. You think she's angry with me? I mean, for coming here...

SOFIA. I think she respects your decision.

NICOLAS. Sometimes I feel guilty about it.

SOFIA. You shouldn't.

NICOLAS. And it didn't put you off?

SOFIA. Sorry?

NICOLAS. When you met him, the fact you knew that he was married and already had a son, it didn't put you off?

SOFIA. I... what do you want me to say, Nicolas?

NICOLAS. Nothing, you're right. I don't know why I'm asking you this kind of question... it's stupid.

SOFIA. No, it's not stupid. It's just...

NICOLAS. Anyway, I have to go. See you later.

(He takes his bag and is gone in a flash. **SOFIA** *finds herself alone, disconcerted by the unpredictability of his changes of mood.)*

SOFIA. See you later.

(Pause. Blackout.)

SIX

(ANNE's flat. End of the afternoon. PIERRE is sitting opposite her. She seems tense.)

ANNE. Well?

PIERRE. Listen, it's going well.

ANNE. Really?

PIERRE. Yes. Quite well. He started at his new school last week. Did he tell you about it?

ANNE. He just left me a message.

PIERRE. He says the atmosphere is quite good.

ANNE. That's good.

PIERRE. Obviously, he didn't much want to go there. I had to apply a bit of pressure... but I think he's getting going again.

ANNE. And was he able to tell you what had happened? I mean...

PIERRE. No. He doesn't say much.

(Pause.)

ANNE. I don't understand where this sadness comes from... it's as if...

PIERRE. He's a teenager, Anne. Have you ever seen a teenager radiating happiness?

ANNE. It's not just that. He's different from the others.

PIERRE. Why do you say that?

ANNE. No reason. I don't know.

> *(Pause.* **PIERRE**'s *mobile rings. He cuts it off.)*

PIERRE. Sorry.

ANNE. What about you? Everything all right in your office? You're working very hard at the moment, if I understand correctly...

PIERRE. Yes.

ANNE. I'm told you're going into politics?

PIERRE. Me? No. One of my clients... Signoret, you know him?

ANNE. *(As if this were proving her point.)* Yes.

PIERRE. He's suggested I join his campaign team. He wants to stand at the primaries. And he's asked me to help him design his platform.

ANNE. You must be pleased.

PIERRE. I'd just be an advisor. I don't even know if I'm going to accept... it's likely to take up a lot of time...

ANNE. When I think that when I met you, you were still a promising young lawyer...

> *(Pause. Embarrassment.)*

PIERRE. But tell me... I'm sorry, I'm coming back to Nicolas... why do you say that? That he's different from the others...

> *(She doesn't answer.)*

He just needs a few rules to be laid down. Don't you think?

ANNE. I don't know.

PIERRE. If you ask me, he's been disappointed in love...

ANNE. You think so?

PIERRE. That's what I've been telling myself. I can't see any other explanation… he's had to split up with a girl and… and there we are. There's nothing abnormal about it, unlike what you're suggesting… in fact, nothing could be more normal. At his age…

ANNE. It's possible. He's so romantic.

PIERRE. Yes.

ANNE. Guess where he gets that from…

(Pause. Embarrassment.)

And what about…

PIERRE. Sofia?

ANNE. Yes. How's she taking it?

(Slight pause.)

You can tell me, you know.

PIERRE. To start with, she was a bit…

ANNE. Hostile, I imagine?

PIERRE. No, not really. Unsettled, perhaps. There's the baby… she's already quite tired. And she hadn't been expecting to be living with a teenager… right off the bat.

ANNE. I can understand.

PIERRE. But all in all, it's going rather well.

ANNE. He's not making life too difficult for her?

PIERRE. No… on the contrary… he's behaving himself. He's making an effort. He's very considerate towards her. There've been some quite happy moments. In fact, I think he likes living with his little brother…

ANNE. Great.

PIERRE. Yes. I think that side of things is going to work.

ANNE. Good.

*(Suddenly, **ANNE** starts crying.)*

PIERRE. Anne... Anne? What's the matter?

ANNE. Nothing. Sorry.

PIERRE. Anne?

(She's trying to hold back the tears, but she breaks down.)

I'm sorry if I ... I didn't want to hurt you.

ANNE. I know.

PIERRE. Why are you crying?

ANNE. I feel as if...

PIERRE. What?

ANNE. I feel as if I've failed completely.

PIERRE. Of course not.

(She goes on crying.)

What are you talking about? Anne? You haven't failed in any way.

ANNE. Sorry. It's just that...

PIERRE. That what?

ANNE. Nothing. Never mind.

(Pause. She recovers.)

I never imagined he'd leave the house. Him as well... And go and live with you.

PIERRE. Me neither, you know. He's the one who asked me.

ANNE. Why didn't he want to live here any more? Does that mean the whole problem started with me? Did it?

PIERRE. Of course not...

ANNE. Yes! If he prefers living somewhere else... and when I phone him, he doesn't even pick up. He never gives me any news... it's as if I don't exist any more. As if... as if he's wiped me out of his life.

PIERRE. Anne... please... when you came to see me, you told me it was very tense between you, that you couldn't manage it any more... that he was making your life a living hell.

ANNE. I know.

PIERRE. You wanted to send him to boarding school, remember?

ANNE. Yes.

PIERRE. You needed a break. Now, you can have more time to yourself.

ANNE. Have more time to myself?

PIERRE. *(Walking on eggshells.)* Yes, I mean... because... I don't know... I've never asked you... you're so discreet...

ANNE. *(Clenched.)* I'm not seeing anyone. If that's what you wanted to know.

> *(Pause. She gets up and moves away from* **PIERRE.***)*

The other day, I came across a photo of him... I found it by accident when I was tidying up and I put it on my bedside table... a photo of him when he was nine. When we went on that safari in Africa... remember?

PIERRE. Yes. Of course.

ANNE. I look at it every morning when I wake up. And every time, I'm devastated... it was taken at dawn... We had to be really quiet so we didn't disturb the lion cubs who were suckling from their mother... do you remember? It was astonishingly beautiful. In the photo, his face is so open... he's like a little sunbeam. Actually, I remember calling him 'my little sunbeam'.

PIERRE. Yes.

ANNE. "My little sunbeam". When you think about it, at that time, everything seemed to be smiling on us. There was so much... yes, joy, in our family. I don't know what happened. Why everything has turned around like this...

PIERRE. Come on...

ANNE. To tell you the truth, I'm afraid this isn't going to end well.

PIERRE. No!... What are you talking about?

ANNE. I don't know. I have like a bad feeling about all this. I loved him so much, you know...

PIERRE. I know.

ANNE. And you as well. I loved you so much, Pierre. If you knew how much I loved you...

(She smiles, at the same time holding back her tears.)

PIERRE. Come on... Don't worry... You're a wonderful mother. You always have been... Mm? It's not your fault if... he's going through a difficult patch, but soon everything will be back to normal.

*(**ANNE** shakes her head.)*

Yes, it will. Believe me, Anne. Everything will be fine and he'll start smiling again. Like in the photo.

(Pause. She dries her tears. Blackout.)

SEVEN

*(**PIERRE**'s flat. Evening. The things are still all over the floor and, once again, everyone behaves as if this chaos didn't exist. **PIERRE** opens a bottle of wine and pours out two glasses. **SOFIA** appears. She looks tired.)*

PIERRE. All right? Is he asleep?

SOFIA. He is. Finally...

PIERRE. He's taken his time...

SOFIA. Yes. I practically fell asleep myself.

PIERRE. Here.

(He hands her a glass.)

SOFIA. Thanks. That's nice. I'm exhausted.

PIERRE. Had a good day?

SOFIA. Nothing special. I went to the paediatrician. Did some shopping. Otherwise, we stayed here. What about you? How was work? Actually, I was wondering... When do you have to give your answer?

PIERRE. Soon.

*(Pause. **PIERRE** smiles.)*

SOFIA. What is it?

PIERRE. Me?

SOFIA. Yes. What is it?

PIERRE. Nothing.

SOFIA. Then why do you look like that?

PIERRE. Like what?

SOFIA. *(With no malice.)* Smug.

> *(He smiles again, amused by **SOFIA**. Pause. Then he puts a box in front of her.)*

What's that?

> *(She takes her time before picking up the box, feigning indifference. Finally, she opens it. It's earrings.)*

What's this in aid of?

PIERRE. Do you like them?

SOFIA. Is this your way of saying sorry?

PIERRE. It's to thank you.

SOFIA. What for?

PIERRE. You know very well.

> *(She looks at him.)*

SOFIA. They're pretty.

PIERRE. You know, I'm well aware... I mean, I'm really grateful for how you've handled all this.

SOFIA. *(Mischievously.)* Yes, that's what I said. It's your way of saying sorry.

PIERRE. What I mean is, it's... lucky you're here.

SOFIA. On the other hand, you're not here much... seems to me you're at work all the time.

PIERRE. Exactly, and I've been thinking about the situation. And I'm not sure I should accept Signoret's offer. It's not come at a good time... what with Nicolas...

SOFIA. You're going to turn it down?

PIERRE. I'm thinking about it.

SOFIA. But you have to accept it, Pierre! You've been talking to me about it for months.

PIERRE. I know.

(**NICOLAS** *appears in his doorway.*)

NICOLAS. Dad? Can I talk to you for a minute?

PIERRE. Yes, of course.

(**NICOLAS** *senses he's interrupted them.*)

NICOLAS. But I'm disturbing you, aren't I?

PIERRE. No, no, not at all. Tell me.

NICOLAS. It's nothing urgent. I just wanted to ask your advice. It can wait... I don't want to interrupt. Will you come and see me afterwards?

PIERRE. Right. I'll join you.

NICOLAS. Great. Thanks.

(*He goes back into his room.*)

PIERRE. Anyway, he looks better. Don't you think? He told me he'd got a very good mark today in philosophy. I think he's starting to regain his self-confidence... I'm so pleased about it... and if I understand correctly, he's been invited out one evening next week...

SOFIA. Has he? That's good.

PIERRE. Yes. Because he needs to see some people. It worries me that he's on his own all the time...

(*Pause.*)

SOFIA. Anyway, it went well.

PIERRE. What?

SOFIA. The paediatrician, with Sacha.

PIERRE. Oh? What did he say?

SOFIA. She. It's a she.

PIERRE. What did she say?

SOFIA. She thinks he'll soon be sleeping through. Like you, she says it's just a "passing phase".

PIERRE. If you ask me, as soon as you go back to work, everything'll be easier. He'll go to the crèche, wear himself out in the normal way during the day, and he'll sleep better at night. Don't you think?

SOFIA. I don't know. Hope so.

(She smiles, but disenchantedly. Pause.)

PIERRE. There's something else I wanted to talk to you about... the week we planned to spend in Italy... beginning of May.

SOFIA. You want to cancel it?

PIERRE. I don't *want* to cancel it. But I'm thinking... might not be the best moment.

*(*SOFIA *says nothing.)*

Not only because of my work... obviously, I hadn't anticipated things would pile up like this... but I was really thinking about Nicolas.

(Pause.)

I know it's important for you... to be able to spend a bit of time together... We all need a rest... but, how to put this? He's only just started back at school... and I'm not sure we should be leaving him here on his own.

SOFIA. Why shouldn't he come with us?

PIERRE. I thought about that, but I'm not sure it's a good idea. He skipped school for months, I don't think I ought to suggest taking him off to the sun when he should be at school...

(Pause.)

I know you're disappointed, but I don't think we have a choice.

SOFIA. I understand.

PIERRE. He needs people around him, you know. It's a decisive moment. That's what I feel and I don't want to leave him just when he's…

SOFIA. *(Interrupting him.)* Pierre, I said I understand. Let's cancel our trip. It's not at all important. We'll go another time.

PIERRE. Are you sure?

SOFIA. Yes.

(He takes her hand.)

PIERRE. Or else… I don't know… you could go without me…

SOFIA. Are they mother-of-pearl? They're really very pretty. I don't suppose I'll have much chance to wear them at the moment, but they're very pretty. Thank you.

*(**SOFIA** looks at him, cold. There's something in the 'thank you' which is not far from resentment, which stops **PIERRE** in his tracks.)*

PIERRE. Are you angry with me?

SOFIA. No. It's just I hadn't actually imagined things turning out like this.

PIERRE. Like what?

(Pause.)

I promise, as soon as Nicolas settles down… we'll go somewhere. We'll go out more often.

SOFIA. I know, it's just a "passing phase".

PIERRE. Why are you saying that?

SOFIA. No reason, sorry. I'm tired. And when I'm tired, I… don't listen to what I'm saying.

>   *(She smiles and takes his hand.)*

Thanks for the present.

>   *(She holds the earrings against her ears to show* **PIERRE** *what they look like.* **PIERRE** *smiles.)*

PIERRE. You remember we're having dinner with Laurent next week?

SOFIA. Yes.

>   *(***PIERRE** *gets up, indicates the earrings.)*

PIERRE. You see, you'll have lots of chances to wear them.

>   *(She smiles to show she's all right, but it's a sad smile.)*

Good. I'm going to see Nicolas. I'll be back soon. All right?

>   *(He crosses the room and knocks on* **NICOLAS***'s door.)*

Nicolas?

>   *(He goes into* **NICOLAS***'s room.* **SOFIA** *is on her own. Music, which might be [***"LORSQUE VOUS N'AUREZ RIEN À FAIRE"***] from Massenet's Chérubin. Pause. She slowly finishes her glass of wine. Then she starts to pick up, one by one, the things that have been lying on the floor since* **NICOLAS***'s apparition. But she does it slowly, with an almost resigned languor, to the rhythm of the melancholy music. This may last some time,*

a kind of visual response to **NICOLAS**'s *first imagined apparition in Scene Three. And little by little, the flat resumes its original appearance. Blackout.)*

EIGHT

(Saturday afternoon. **NICOLAS** *is wearing a new jacket and looking at himself in the mirror.)*

PIERRE. Well?

NICOLAS. I'm not sure.

PIERRE. Well, I think it suits you.

NICOLAS. Do you? I don't look a bit...

PIERRE. A bit what?

NICOLAS. I don't know. I feel sort of ridiculous.

PIERRE. I'm telling you, it's perfect.

*(***NICOLAS*** looks at himself in the mirror.)*

I was walking past this shop, I saw it in the window... And I thought you'd like it. You did tell me you were going out one evening next week, didn't you? You'll need something to wear...

NICOLAS. It's nice of you, but...

PIERRE. What?

NICOLAS. I'm not sure people my age wear jackets...

PIERRE. Are you joking? The salesman, for example... hardly older than you... he was wearing one...

NICOLAS. Was he?

PIERRE. He told me everyone was wearing them now. And, honestly, it suits you. Makes you look stylish.

NICOLAS. You know, I'm not even sure I'm going to this party…

PIERRE. Why not?

    (**NICOLAS** *shrugs his shoulders.*)

You have to go. It's important, seeing people… having a bit of fun… opening yourself up to others… you can't spend all your time on your own…

NICOLAS. I know. But I don't feel very close to people my own age. They're really stupid, you know. For example, they all can't wait to be eighteen, as if that's going to change anything… fine, have a party to celebrate. But what use is it, being eighteen? None. To be able to go clubbing? I couldn't care less about clubbing. It doesn't interest me.

PIERRE. So what does interest you?

    (**NICOLAS** *shrugs his shoulders.*)

NICOLAS. I'd have liked never to be my age. It's too complicated for me. Too many responsibilities. Too much pressure. I preferred it when I was a child. Anyway, I don't know how to dance.

PIERRE. Ah, so that's the problem…

NICOLAS. I'll just be standing in a corner watching everyone else…

PIERRE. All you have to do is ask Sofia to teach you… she's the best dancer I know…

    (*On cue,* **SOFIA** *appears.*)

SOFIA. What are you talking about?

PIERRE. I was just telling Nicolas you're a great dancer.

SOFIA. Very funny.

    (**PIERRE** *smiles.*)

(To **PIERRE.***)* Given the way you dance, you have the nerve to criticise me?

(**NICOLAS** *smiles in his turn.*)

NICOLAS. *(To* **SOFIA.***)* Why? Isn't he a good dancer?

SOFIA. Let's just say he has his own style.

PIERRE. My unique style.

SOFIA. Did you know we met at a wedding?

NICOLAS. No, I didn't.

PIERRE. Sofia…

SOFIA. Everyone was dancing and that was my first sight of your father. He was on the floor, doing his famous hip-sway.

NICOLAS. *(Big smile.)* What's that?

SOFIA. You don't know your father's famous hip-sway?

NICOLAS. No.

PIERRE. Sofia… Better you just teach him to dance… he's going to a party next week.

SOFIA. *(To* **NICOLAS.***)* Watch.

PIERRE. What are you doing?

(She goes and puts on some music. **NICOLAS** is smiling broadly.)*

SOFIA. Come on… Pierre… aren't you going to show us?

PIERRE. Is this really a good idea?

---

* A licence to produce THE SON does not include a performance licence for any third-party or copyrighted music. Licensees should create an original composition or use music in the public domain. For further information, please see Music Use Note on page iii.

(SOFIA indicates 'yes', pretending to be annoyed.)

I'm afraid to wake Sacha…

NICOLAS. Come on, Dad!

PIERRE. All right. At your own risk. You asked for it…

(He starts dancing to the music. SOFIA and NICOLAS burst out laughing. PIERRE exaggerates to make them laugh more.)

SOFIA. You see why I immediately fell in love with him…

NICOLAS. Who wouldn't?

PIERRE. I know, I'm irresistible.

SOFIA. When he starts, everyone else stops dancing. He can't help drawing attention to himself.

NICOLAS. How do you do it?

PIERRE. Like this, look…

(NICOLAS starts dancing himself, imitating his father's movements.)

NICOLAS. Like this?

SOFIA. Oh! No! Don't tell me… not another one?

PIERRE. That's it! Marvellous! That's all you need for your party!

SOFIA. You'll knock them dead…

PIERRE. Now I recognise my son! Look at him move! That's my son!

(SOFIA laughs and PIERRE dances with NICOLAS. Then SOFIA starts dancing as well. They dance for a while. They might even join in with the lyrics. Joyous atmosphere. Suddenly, NICOLAS breaks off and stops

moving. Something has totally taken over his thoughts. An intense sadness seems to engulf him. He heads towards his room, leaving the others in the middle of their dance.)

Nicolas?

*(**NICOLAS** leaves. **SOFIA** goes to turn off the music.)*

SOFIA. What's the matter with him?

PIERRE. I don't know.

*(**PIERRE** goes over to **NICOLAS**'s door.)*

Nicolas?

(The door's been locked.)

Nicolas? What's the matter?

SOFIA. Did we say something?

PIERRE. Nicolas? Open this door... Nicolas?

(Pause. Blackout.)

NINE

(It's a Sunday, but **PIERRE** *is working. The flat is back to its original appearance.* **SOFIA** *is settling the baby into the pushchair. She's getting ready to go out to the park with Sacha.)*

SOFIA. Pierre? Can I talk to you for a minute?

*(***PIERRE** *has his head in a file.)*

PIERRE. Mm?

SOFIA. Can I talk to you?

PIERRE. Are you going out?

SOFIA. Yes. But I just wanted a word with you before I... if it isn't too much of a distraction...

PIERRE. Yes?

(Pause. **PIERRE** *looks up from the file.)*

What's going on?

SOFIA. I know you're working, but... this is important.

(Brief pause.)

Just now, I ... well, I was just tidying Nicolas's things. I was just doing his room and... not sure how to put this... I –

PIERRE. Tell me.

SOFIA. I found a knife.

PIERRE. What?

SOFIA. Just a kitchen knife... all the same.

PIERRE. In his room?

SOFIA. Yes.

PIERRE. What's all this about?

SOFIA. It was hidden under his mattress. I took it away, obviously. But I was thinking you ought to speak to him about it...

(**PIERRE** *exhales and puts down his file.*)

I'm sorry. I thought I'd better tell you.

PIERRE. Why did he take a knife?

SOFIA. I don't know.

PIERRE. You think he's...

(*He indicates his forearms.*)

I don't understand. Why does he do that? I thought he... he seems to be doing well, doesn't he?

(**SOFIA** *shrugs her shoulders.*)

Don't you think?

SOFIA. I don't know.

PIERRE. He's going to school, he's smiling, he's... he's better.

SOFIA. Yes.

PIERRE. So? Why is he doing this?

SOFIA. I think the simplest thing would be to talk to him about it.

(*Pause.*)

Don't make that face.

PIERRE. Sorry. Yes. You're right. You... are you leaving?

SOFIA. Yes. While the weather's still nice. I'm not suggesting you come with us...

PIERRE. No, that's nice of you. I have to prepare this file for Monday.

SOFIA. But we're going to get a bit of sun. Aren't we, my little man?

> *(She notices that **PIERRE** is still lost in thought.)*

Don't worry. He's bound to still be a bit fragile... we mustn't over-dramatise. And you're right, he's better, thanks to everything you're doing for him.

> *(**PIERRE** doesn't know what to think about this. He's suddenly racked with doubt.)*

PIERRE. Do you think so?

> *(**NICOLAS** appears in his bedroom door.)*

Ah. Nicolas...

NICOLAS. You going for a walk in the park?

SOFIA. Just Sacha and me. Your father's staying here. He has work to do.

PIERRE. Anyway, I wanted a word with you before I get back to it...

NICOLAS. Now?

PIERRE. Yes.

NICOLAS. What about?

SOFIA. In that case, we'll leave you... all right?

PIERRE. Yes. See you soon, darling. Have a nice walk.

SOFIA. See you soon.

> *(She goes out with the pushchair.)*

NICOLAS. What's going on?

> *(Pause.)*

Is there a problem?

PIERRE. Yes.

> *(Brief pause. **PIERRE** searches for a way to introduce this delicate topic.)*

Why have you hidden a knife under your mattress?

NICOLAS. What?

PIERRE. There's a knife under your mattress. You know about this?

> *(Brief pause.)*

What's it doing there?

NICOLAS. Nothing.

PIERRE. What do you mean, "nothing"?

NICOLAS. It's just there. In case.

PIERRE. In case of what? What are you talking about?

NICOLAS. I don't know. If there was a burglar… or… makes me feel safer.

> *(Pause. He's well aware his father is not convinced by this explanation.)*

The other night, I thought I… I heard a noise, even though there was no one there. For a moment, I was afraid. Sometimes, I get a bit paranoid… No need to make a fuss about it.

> *(Pause.)*

PIERRE. Show me your arm.

NICOLAS. What?

PIERRE. Show me your arm.

NICOLAS. No.

> (**PIERRE** *grabs hold of his arm and sees that there are recent scars.*)

PIERRE. Nicolas...

> (*They look at each other for a moment without speaking.*)

Why do you do this?

NICOLAS. Do what?

PIERRE. You know very well.

> (**NICOLAS** *shrugs his shoulders.*)

Explain it to me. Why do you do this?

NICOLAS. I don't know.

> (**PIERRE** *seems irritated by these perpetual refusals to answer.*)

PIERRE. I don't want you to hurt yourself. Do you understand me?

NICOLAS. I don't hurt myself.

PIERRE. Have you seen these scars? That's what I call hurting yourself.

NICOLAS. It's the opposite.

PIERRE. What do you mean, the opposite?

NICOLAS. Nothing.

PIERRE. No, explain it to me. Explain it to me, Nicolas.

> (**NICOLAS** *tries to find an explanation.*)

NICOLAS. It relieves me.

PIERRE. Relieves you of what?

(NICOLAS *shrugs his shoulders.*)

Relieves you of what?

NICOLAS. When I'm in pain, I... It's a way to channel the pain...

PIERRE. But what pain?

(*Pause.*)

(*Perturbed.*) Nicolas... a way to channel what pain?

(*Pause.* PIERRE *pulls himself together.*)

I don't want you to do it any more.

NICOLAS. But...

PIERRE. It's not up for discussion. I forbid you to do this. Is that clear?

(*Pause.*)

Nicolas. Is that clear?

NICOLAS. Yes.

PIERRE. I don't accept this way of... there are things in life you don't do. I mean, do you realise? With a knife?

NICOLAS. Was it Sofia who found it?

PIERRE. Doesn't matter.

NICOLAS. What's she doing searching through my things?

PIERRE. She's not searching through your things. She was kind enough to make your bed. As you never make it yourself!

NICOLAS. (*Trying to gloss things over in adolescent fashion.*) Oh, come on...

PIERRE. What?

NICOLAS. It's not as if…

PIERRE. *(Interrupting him.)* It's not as if what? You admit you took a knife out of the kitchen so you could…

NICOLAS. I didn't take it for that originally. I just told you. I just wanted to have a knife with me. To defend myself.

PIERRE. Defend yourself? Defend yourself from what? What are you talking about? You realise this makes no sense at all?

NICOLAS. Well, you have a gun!

PIERRE. What?

NICOLAS. In the utility room, behind the cupboard, there's a gun.

PIERRE. Mm? Yes, but… that's… that's got nothing to do with it. It's…

> (**NICOLAS** *watches him, waiting for him to complete the sentence.*)

It was a present.

NICOLAS. A present?

PIERRE. Yes. But that's got nothing to do with it. It has nothing to do with our discussion, Nicolas.

NICOLAS. Who gave you a gun?

> (**PIERRE** *clearly doesn't want to go into the details, but he feels obliged to offer some explanation.*)

PIERRE. My father. A long time ago. He loved hunting. It was his passion. It's a hunting rifle. See, there's nothing out of the ordinary about it. It's not there so I can "defend myself".

NICOLAS. Why did he give you a hunting rifle?

PIERRE. To… he must have thought I'd like it. That it was something we could do together. That… but, you know,

I never used it. I loathe hunting. And everything that goes with it.

NICOLAS. So why do you keep it?

PIERRE. If you must know, I'd forgotten I had it... It was in the cellar for years. I found it when... the time when I moved... and I stuck it behind the cupboard... for the time being. Because the flat doesn't have a cellar... as stupid as that.

NICOLAS. Is it loaded?

PIERRE. Nicolas... this is not what we're talking about.

(Brief pause.)

Why do you do this sort of thing? Honestly, I don't understand...

NICOLAS. I know.

(Pause.)

PIERRE. What happened at your last school?

*(**NICOLAS** doesn't answer.)*

This might be the time to tell me about it, don't you think?

(Pause.)

Something must have happened... otherwise, you wouldn't have this kind of... you wouldn't do these things.

(Pause.)

I won't be able to understand, if you don't say anything... I'm here to help you, Nicolas.

(Pause.)

If you don't want to talk to me about it, maybe there's someone else you could talk to… what do you think?

NICOLAS. I don't want to talk about it.

> *(Pause.)*

PIERRE. Anyway, if you're in pain, there are other ways to channel it. Why have you given up sport? You ought to go running in the park! We could go together if you like. On Saturday mornings… or whenever you like! But this, this is unacceptable. Do you understand?

> *(Brief pause.* **PIERRE** *takes* **NICOLAS***'s arms.)*

I'm going to give you some disinfectant.

NICOLAS. No, no… it's just scratches.

> *(Brief pause.* **PIERRE** *makes an affectionate gesture towards* **NICOLAS***.)*

PIERRE. You know, when you hurt yourself, it's as if you were doing it to me.

NICOLAS. *(Cold, reproachful.)* And when you hurt Mum, you were doing it to me.

> *(***PIERRE** *is caught offguard. Pause. Blackout.)*

TEN

(A Saturday evening. **PIERRE**'s *doing up his tie in front of the mirror in the drawing room. Behind him,* **NICOLAS** *arrives with a bowl of cereal and settles down on the sofa.)*

PIERRE. You eating cereal?

NICOLAS. Yes.

PIERRE. You wouldn't like to try something a bit more exciting?

*(***NICOLAS*** looks at him uncomprehendingly.)*

I don't know, it's Saturday evening…

NICOLAS. So?

PIERRE. Don't you want to see your friends?… Or go to the cinema? …

NICOLAS. I don't have any friends.

PIERRE. Why say that?

NICOLAS. Because it's the truth.

(Brief pause.)

PIERRE. You used to have… Sebastien. You used to see him a lot. And… what was he called? Mathieu… the one with the long hair… why don't you see them any more?

(Pause.)

And what about that party you told me about…?

NICOLAS. All right… Dad…

PIERRE. What?

NICOLAS. Can you stop now?

> (**SOFIA** *comes into the room. She's wearing a dress.*)

SOFIA. You haven't seen my earrings, have you, darling? I had them in my hand just now... since when they've disappeared...

PIERRE. Mm? No. Have you looked in the bedroom?

SOFIA. I've looked everywhere... I can't understand it. I'm losing my marbles.

> (**PIERRE**'s *mobile rings.*)

PIERRE. Ah... just a minute. Hello? Yes... yes...

> (*He goes out.* **SOFIA** *puts on lipstick, looking at herself in the mirror.*)

SOFIA. You haven't seen them?

NICOLAS. What?

SOFIA. My mother-of-pearl earrings... The ones your father gave me... they were around here somewhere a minute ago...

NICOLAS. No.

SOFIA. I keep losing things at the moment...

> (*Pause.*)

NICOLAS. You changed your dress? That one really suits you.

SOFIA. That's a nice thing to say.

NICOLAS. No, it's true. You look beautiful.

> (**SOFIA** *smiles.*)

Where are you going?

SOFIA. Nowhere particularly special... dinner with some friends... Laurent, do you know him?

NICOLAS. No.

SOFIA. Well, I say "nowhere particularly special", but in fact it is pretty special... It's practically the first time we've gone out since Sacha was born... some good advice, if you want to go on having a life, don't have a child!

> *(She smiles, but immediately thinks better of it.)*

I'm joking.

NICOLAS. You know, I know you... I mean, you didn't choose to live with me... and I ... I do... I appreciate the fact you... because you weren't against my moving in here...

SOFIA. Why should I be against it?

NICOLAS. I don't know.

SOFIA. You're Sacha's brother. So it's your home as well here.

NICOLAS. Yes.

> *(**NICOLAS** looks sad. Suddenly, **SOFIA** has an idea.)*

SOFIA. Are you still thinking about that girl?

> *(**NICOLAS** looks at her, astonished.)*

Your father told me... what I mean is... he told me you'd finally explained to him what happened... at your old school.

NICOLAS. What did he tell you?

SOFIA. He just said... I mean, that you'd had this girlfriend and that you'd broken up...

(Pause.)

(Kindly.) Don't worry. In the end, we forget these things.

(Suddenly, **PIERRE** *comes in.)*

PIERRE. Right. Bad news... Laetitia's stood us up.

SOFIA. What?

PIERRE. I've just had her on the phone.

SOFIA. But... just now? At the last minute?

PIERRE. She's ill.

SOFIA. Is this a joke?

PIERRE. I'm sorry.

SOFIA. She might at least have said a bit sooner.

PIERRE. She was really apologetic, but she has a temperature...

SOFIA. Yes, but just like that, at the last minute... what are we going to do?

NICOLAS. Who's Laetitia?

PIERRE. The young woman who was going to look after Sacha this evening.

SOFIA. Should I call Marie?

PIERRE. I already have. She's not free.

SOFIA. Great. The one time we were able to go out!

PIERRE. What shall I do? Call Laurent? Cancel?

*(***SOFIA*** exhales.)*

NICOLAS. You want me to look after him?

PIERRE. You?

NICOLAS. If you like. I could take care of things.

PIERRE. You... you think you could manage it?

NICOLAS. *(As if it were self-evident.)* Yes.

(**SOFIA** *is hesitating.*)

PIERRE. What do you...?

SOFIA. No, it's kind of you, but...

PIERRE. Why not?

SOFIA. No. You know, he's only a baby. It's...

NICOLAS. It's your decision... I only suggested it to help you out...

SOFIA. It's very sweet of you. But I think it would be better if...

PIERRE. Are you sure? Because...

SOFIA. Yes. Very nice. Call Laurent. We'd better cancel.

NICOLAS. Just as you like.

(**NICOLAS** *leaves.* **PIERRE** *looks daggers at* **SOFIA.**)

SOFIA. What?

PIERRE. Nothing.

SOFIA. Why are you looking at me like that?

PIERRE. Why do you think? He made a kind suggestion... I don't know why you're refusing.

SOFIA. You don't see why?

PIERRE. No. He's his little brother.

SOFIA. So?

PIERRE. So he can look after him.

SOFIA. I'm just not sure. He's only a baby, and...

PIERRE. And what?

(Pause.)

You always see things in such a black light.

SOFIA. Better to see them in a black light than not to see them at all.

PIERRE. What do you mean?

SOFIA. Nothing.

PIERRE. Yes. Tell me... what am I not seeing?

SOFIA. Never mind.

PIERRE. You really believe Nicolas is not capable of looking after his little brother while he's asleep?

(She doesn't answer.)

You have to trust him, Sofia. Otherwise how is he going to recover?

SOFIA. He's... You know very well. He's coming out of a depression. He's still unstable. And he's even... I'm sorry if this shocks you... but I'm not trusting my son to...

PIERRE. To...?

*(She doesn't answer. **NICOLAS** appears in the doorway. He's holding the earrings in his hand. But **PIERRE** and **SOFIA** aren't aware of his presence.)*

Go on, say it. You're not trusting your son to...

SOFIA. Stop it.

PIERRE. Say it.

SOFIA. He's weird, Pierre. Don't say he isn't. In fact, he's ultra-weird. The look in his eyes, it's worrying sometimes. He... I mean, let's face it, open your eyes, he's not right in the head!

(Suddenly **SOFIA** *becomes aware of* **NICOLAS**. **PIERRE**, *seeing* **SOFIA**'s *aghast expression, turns towards* **NICOLAS**.*)*

PIERRE. Nicolas... you... what are you doing?

(Pause.)

Nicolas? You... ah, you've found the earrings.

SOFIA. Where were they?

(Pause. **NICOLAS** *doesn't move.)*

PIERRE. Nicolas... you mustn't think... we were arguing because... well, you understand the situation... It's nothing to do with you... we were just disappointed about not being able to go out tonight... do you understand? Sofia got a bit over-excited, she wasn't thinking about what she was saying. Do you hear what I'm saying?

(Pause.)

Nicolas? I'm speaking to you...

*(***NICOLAS** *moves slowly towards* **SOFIA** *and hands her the earrings.)*

NICOLAS. They were out in the corridor.

(He half turns towards his room.)

PIERRE. Nicolas?

(He doesn't turn back.)

Nicolas?

(He leaves. **PIERRE** *and* **SOFIA** *are alone in the room.* **PIERRE** *takes a painful breath. Then he aims a black look, full of reproach, at* **SOFIA**. *Blackout.)*

ELEVEN

(**ANNE**'s *flat.* **NICOLAS** *is on his own. He's writing in an exercise book. Suddenly, the door opens and* **ANNE** *appears. Seeing* **NICOLAS** *makes her jump.*)

ANNE. Nicolas? You gave me a fright... what are you doing here?

> (*Pause.*)

You... you should have told me you were coming by. I... I didn't know.

> (*She comes up to him and greets him.*)

Are you all right?

NICOLAS. What about you?

ANNE. I'm happy to see you. You... were you waiting for me?

> (**NICOLAS** *shrugs his shoulders.*)

What's the matter?

NICOLAS. Nothing. I wanted to talk to you.

ANNE. Do you have a bit of time? What time is it? Shouldn't you be at school?

NICOLAS. I was just in the area.

ANNE. Would you like something to drink or...?

NICOLAS. No, thanks.

> (*She sits down.*)

ANNE. How are you? I've left you I don't know how many messages but you never answer... tell me. Are you all right?

NICOLAS. So-so. That's why I came. I wanted to ask you...

ANNE. What?

NICOLAS. I mean, I wanted to know... in fact, I've changed my mind.

ANNE. What about?

NICOLAS. About... do you think I could come back and live here?

ANNE. Here? But why? I mean... aren't things going well?

(**NICOLAS** *shrugs his shoulders.*)

I thought everything was going well. Your father told me you were happy at your new school... aren't you?

(Pause.)

Why don't you ever answer me? I left so many messages on your voicemail and...

NICOLAS. I know. I'm sorry...

ANNE. Are you angry with me?

NICOLAS. No.

(Pause.)

ANNE. Towards the end, things got difficult between us. It's true. But, you know, I'm so happy you've come here to talk to me. I've missed you.

NICOLAS. I've missed you too.

(She smiles.)

ANNE. Why do you want to come back here? ... I mean, it's your home... that's your room. But I mean... have you discussed this with your father?

NICOLAS. No.

> *(Pause.)*

ANNE. What's going on, Nicolas?

NICOLAS. I don't feel good, over there. I was hoping… I thought…

> *(He can't finish his sentence.)*

But in the end, there's no room for me.

ANNE. Why do you say that? I thought your father was saying…

NICOLAS. They find me disturbing more than anything else. I can see it now. I disturb them. And he puts so much pressure on me.

ANNE. Your father?

NICOLAS. Yes. He doesn't realise, but he never stops talking to me about my school work. As if that's all there was to life…

ANNE. It's normal. He worries about you.

NICOLAS. No. He doesn't give a shit about me. I mean, about who I really am. He just wants me to succeed, like him. The way he has. But I have no desire to be a law student or to become a lawyer. I couldn't give a shit. It doesn't interest me.

ANNE. I know.

> *(Pause.)*

At one time, your dream was to be a writer.

NICOLAS. Yes.

> *(She smiles at him.)*

ANNE. Are you still writing?

(**NICOLAS** *shrugs his shoulders but in a way that implies the answer "yes".*)

You remind me of my brother. Both of you are artists.

NICOLAS. I never said that. Anyway, he went into insurance. So thanks for the comparison...

(She smiles.)

ANNE. That's right. I always felt he'd missed out... he could have done great things, I'm sure of it. If he'd persevered... and so could you.

(Pause.)

NICOLAS. Anyway, I'm not feeling good over there. I don't think I'll ever be up to standard.

ANNE. Don't say that...

NICOLAS. It's true. I feel so worthless... I can see what he thinks of me. I can see it from his side. Even if he denies it... and I don't want to disappoint him.

ANNE. What are you talking about?

(Pause.)

Your father wants the best for you, Nicolas. It's just you're very different. And I suspect that at the moment he's also under a lot of pressure. Don't you think? You mustn't hold it against him. This business... has he talked to you about it?

NICOLAS. About what?

ANNE. He's going to help Signoret draw up his economic plan. He's been dreaming about doing this for years. It's important to him. His father was in politics. He was a town councillor for years, did you know?

NICOLAS. No.

ANNE. I suspect there's some connection. In some way, he wants to poach on his territory...

NICOLAS. Did you know he'd given him a gun?

ANNE. Mm?

NICOLAS. Speaking of poaching... he told me he'd given him a gun.

ANNE. Maybe. I don't know.

NICOLAS. He still has it at the flat... I've seen it. He says he loathes hunting. But when he says it, you get the feeling that it's actually his father that he loathes.

(**ANNE** *smiles, confirming this.*)

Why weren't they on speaking terms?

ANNE. It's a long story... your grandfather was a very... unusual man.

NICOLAS. Meaning?

ANNE. He showed no generosity to Pierre. He was very absent... and he never encouraged him. That's the thing, when you tell me your father's putting pressure on you... he's trying to do what's best. In his own way. But he believes in you. He loves you.

(*Pause.*)

NICOLAS. I'll never manage it.

ANNE. Why do you say that?

(*Brief pause.* **NICOLAS** *hesitates to confide anymore.*)

NICOLAS. I ...

ANNE. Why can't you manage it?

NICOLAS. I'm not well, Mum.

(**ANNE** *is thinking about the romantic break-up* **PIERRE** *has talked to her about. She smiles gently at him. She'd like to show that she understands his unhappiness.*)

ANNE. Your father told me you'd broken up with a girl. Is that it?

(Brief pause.)

That's not it.

NICOLAS. No.

ANNE. All the same...

NICOLAS. *(Interrupting her.)* Yes, I know. That's what I told him.

*(**ANNE** looks at him uncomprehendingly.)*

He didn't understand what was wrong... he needed a rational explanation. You know what he's like... so I told him what he wanted to hear.

ANNE. You mean...

NICOLAS. I never even went out with that girl.

*(Pause. **ANNE** still doesn't understand.)*

It's just...

(Brief pause.)

It's just I'm not made like other people.

*(**ANNE** looks at him questioningly. What does he mean?)*

Sometimes I feel I'm not made for this life. I can't manage it. Even so, I try, every day, with all my strength, but I can't manage it. I'm in pain, permanently. And I'm tired. I'm tired of being in pain.

ANNE. Nicolas...

NICOLAS. I want it to end, Mum.

*(**ANNE** seems very upset. She takes him in her arms.)*

ANNE. Don't say that, my love. Never say that. Do you understand me? You have so much ahead of you. You have your whole life... so don't say that, my little sunbeam... Do you understand me? Don't say that to your mother.

> *(She caresses him, maternally. He closes his eyes. Pause. Blackout.)*

TWELVE

(The apartment. Afternoon. **PIERRE** *arrives back from his office. He goes directly to* **NICOLAS**'s *door and knocks.)*

PIERRE. Nicolas! Could you come here, please?

NICOLAS. *(Offstage.)* What is it?

PIERRE. Come here! I need to talk to you.

*(***PIERRE** *crosses the room. He's clearly tense.* **NICOLAS** *appears in his doorway.)*

NICOLAS. What?

PIERRE. Sit down.

NICOLAS. What is it?

PIERRE. I said, sit down. We need to talk.

*(***NICOLAS** *sits down.)*

I'm going to try to speak calmly, but I'm not sure I'll manage it. Because I'm very angry.

(Pause.)

What's going on?

*(***NICOLAS** *doesn't know what he's talking about.)*

You obviously don't know what I'm talking about.

NICOLAS. No.

PIERRE. I'm talking about school... what's going on?

NICOLAS. Nothing special. Why?

PIERRE. Nothing special?

NICOLAS. No.

> *(Pause. It's clear that* **PIERRE** *is trying to restrain himself.)*

PIERRE. Yesterday afternoon you had your mock exam, is that right?

NICOLAS. Yes.

PIERRE. That's what you told me. How did it go?

NICOLAS. I've already told you.

PIERRE. Yes, but I'd like you to tell me again.

NICOLAS. Quite well. I think.

PIERRE. Good.

> *(Brief pause.)*

Only, you see, yesterday afternoon, Sofia went for a walk with Sacha. They went to the park and they saw you. You were sitting on a bench. Apparently, you were writing in an exercise book. In any case, you weren't at school.

> *(Pause.)*

So I'm going to ask you one last time and this time I want an answer... what's going on?

> *(Pause.)*

You've started to skip classes again, is that it?

NICOLAS. No.

PIERRE. Then why weren't you at school yesterday?

NICOLAS. Why did she tell you that?

PIERRE. That's not the problem, Nicolas.

NICOLAS. Yes, it is the problem.

PIERRE. No! It is not the problem. The problem is that we're doing everything we can to help you, that we're trying to do our best for you, that we're bending over backwards for your sake, while at the same time you're taking us for... you're taking the piss!

NICOLAS. She told you because she wants to set us against one another.

PIERRE. That's not true.

NICOLAS. Since the start, she's wanted me out of here.

PIERRE. You're wrong. And anyway, that's not what we're talking about. Whether she's said that to me or not is not the problem! The problem is that you're lying to me, Nicolas. Why weren't you at school yesterday?

(Pause.)

I'm listening.

NICOLAS. I didn't feel well. I... I couldn't bring myself to go. I'm under too much pressure because of this exam and I... I'm sorry.

PIERRE. You're sorry?

(Pause.)

I called the school. I called them. And you know what they told me?

(Pause.)

They told me you'd never been back there.

*(**NICOLAS** lowers his eyes. Pause.)*

They told me you were there on the first day, two months ago, and afterwards, you never came back. Never. Not once.

(Pause.)

They said they'd been sending letters. You're not saying anything?

(Pause.)

When I think you had the nerve to tell me you were getting good marks and being invited to parties and... The whole time, you were lying to me!

(Pause.)

Now what am I supposed to do? Send you to boarding school?

(**NICOLAS** *gives a strange smile, as if what* **PIERRE** *has said is predictable.*)

What sort of a reaction were you expecting from me? What have you been doing all these days? Because I can't understand what benefit you... you were walking, is that it? You...

(**PIERRE** *seems at a loss.*)

We give you a chance to climb back up the slope and what do you do? You carry on just as before. You... you lie to everybody... you...

(He can't find anything else to say. Pause.)

Explain it to me! What's going on? Are you on drugs?

(*This makes* **NICOLAS** *smile.*)

Well, then, explain it to me!

(Pause.)

Because I don't know what else to do with you. I'm telling you honestly, I just don't know... I've tried to listen to you, to stand shoulder to shoulder, to give you strength and confidence, but evidently, none of that's any use.

(*Pause.*)

You think you can live your life like that? Just doing what you feel like? Getting out of going to school, of taking any responsibility, of growing up... what are you going to do with your life? If you're not doing anything! Tell me, what's to become of you?

(*Pause.* **NICOLAS** *says nothing, but is staring at him.*)

Obviously, you have no answer. And stop staring at me like that. What's the idea? To intimidate me. That won't work, I can tell you right away. Not with me.

(*Pause.*)

All right, I'm going to explain to you how things are going to be. From tomorrow on, whether you like it or not, you're going back to school. Is that clear?

NICOLAS. No.

PIERRE. Sorry?

NICOLAS. (*Calmly.*) I'm saying no, I will not go back to school.

(*Pause.*)

PIERRE. What are you playing at, Nicolas?

(*Pause.*)

When I was your age, my mother was ill, I didn't see my father anymore, I had money problems, but I fought on. I fought on and, believe me, most days it wasn't much fun. And what's happened to you? What is there in your life that's so dramatic you're not able to go to school like everybody else? Answer me!

(Pause.)

Answer me, Nicolas!

NICOLAS. I can't manage it.

PIERRE. You can't manage it? I don't even understand what that means. You can't manage what? Getting up in the morning? Concentrating? Making an effort?

NICOLAS. Living.

(Brief pause.)

I can't manage living. And it's your fault.

PIERRE. Sorry?

NICOLAS. If I'm like this. It's your fault.

PIERRE. What are you talking about?

(Pause.)

What's my fault? What have I done? Tell me.

NICOLAS. You disgust me.

PIERRE. Sorry?

(Pause.)

What did you say?

NICOLAS. You make all these grand speeches about life and work, then you abandon us as if we were pieces of shit without a second glance...

PIERRE. What?

NICOLAS. You give yourself these superior airs, but since the start you've basically behaved like a bastard.

*(**PIERRE** is trying to keep calm.)*

PIERRE. Take back what you just said! Nicolas... do you hear me? Take back what you just said, at once!

NICOLAS. Bastard!

> (**PIERRE** *cracks and launches himself at* **NICOLAS**. *He grabs him by the scruff of the neck and shakes him as he speaks.*)

PIERRE. Me, a bastard? Me?

> (**NICOLAS** *tries to struggle free, but* **PIERRE** *keeps a grip on him.*)

I've taken care of you all these years! Have you wanted for anything at all? Have I not always done everything for you? Answer me!

> (*But he won't answer.* **PIERRE** *raises his voice, he's practically in tears and he shakes his son more and more violently, in desperation.*)

Answer, for Christ's sake!

> (**PIERRE** *goes on, more and more desperately and it turns into an increasingly physical struggle.*)

For years, you hear me... I've looked after you. I stayed with your mother... so why are you saying this? Why?

NICOLAS. Let me go!

PIERRE. Is it because I fell in love with another woman? Is that it? Is that my crime? What business is it of yours? Mm? I have the right to reinvent my life. Shit! It's my life! You hear me?

> (**PIERRE** *is almost shouting.*)

It's my life!

> (*They both collapse on the floor. Pause.* **NICOLAS** *is as if paralysed; he never thought his father would react so violently.* **PIERRE** *also seems shell-shocked. He gets his breath*

back and controls himself. Pause. **PIERRE** *reaches for* **NICOLAS**'s *shoulder, as if he wanted to pacify him, but then moves away to let the tension dissipate. He has some difficulty getting his breath back. He wipes away his tears and tries to calm down.* **NICOLAS** *still hasn't moved. He's like a six-year-old, terrified. Then,* **PIERRE** *turns back to* **NICOLAS**.)

I'm sorry, Nicolas. I don't know what came over me.

(*He wants to help him get up, but* **NICOLAS** *snatches away, gets up on his own and looks at* **PIERRE** *with horror. Then he heads for the front door of the flat.*)

Nicolas?

(**NICOLAS** *doesn't turn back.*)

Nicolas, please...

(**NICOLAS** *leaves, slamming the door. Pause.* **PIERRE** *looks totally lost. Blackout.*)

THIRTEEN

(Waiting room in an emergency ward. **PIERRE** *is anxiously waiting. Suddenly,* **ANNE** *appears. It looks as if she's been running.)*

PIERRE. Anne...

ANNE. Where is he?

PIERRE. They're with him. Don't worry.

ANNE. How is he? Have they told you anything?

PIERRE. They found him in time. Everything's going to be all right.

(She embraces him tightly.)

ANNE. God... what's happened?

PIERRE. The doctor's coming to see us. He'll explain. Don't worry.

ANNE. But you're sure there's no danger?

PIERRE. So they told me.

ANNE. My little boy...

PIERRE. Come on, it's almost over. It'll be all right...

ANNE. But what happened? What did he do it with?

PIERRE. A razor.

ANNE. He told me the other day. He told me he wanted to... I should have listened to him... or understood him better.

PIERRE. Come on... calm down.

ANNE. It's my fault. He came to see me. He came to talk to me and he... told me quite plainly.

PIERRE. Anne, please, calm down... everything's all right. Do you understand me?

ANNE. No, everything's not all right! How can you say that? And why doesn't he have an electric razor?

> (**PIERRE** *takes her in his arms to calm her down.*)

PIERRE. Come on... calm down. Please... calm down. It's no use getting into a state. Please...

> (*Pause. She calms down.*)

ANNE. How long do we have to wait?

PIERRE. I don't know.

ANNE. How long have you been here?

PIERRE. Half an hour, something like that. They told me they'd be out to see us soon.

ANNE. But why did he do that?

> (*She senses that* **PIERRE** *is hesitant to answer.*)

What happened?

PIERRE. I wasn't there. I was working. It was Sofia who found him. She called an ambulance and they brought him here. I came right away.

ANNE. But didn't she say anything to you?

PIERRE. No. All I know is, she... she went out and... she'd forgotten her mobile and she had to go back to the house. That's how she found him in the bathroom... He'd just... we were lucky. The ambulance arrived very quickly... I'm sorry. I'm really sorry.

ANNE. I don't understand.

PIERRE. It's more than ten days since… since our fight… He told you about it, I expect? He hardly ever left the flat. He was going round in circles. He wasn't doing anything. It was hell. For everyone else, as well.

ANNE. I know.

PIERRE. After it happened, his attitude towards me changed… he hardly ever answered me, he wouldn't look me in the eye… I'm telling you, it got really unbearable. And yesterday evening, I lost my temper… d'you understand? I can't get rid of this constant feeling of rage… I want to shake him! He has everything anyone needs to be happy. Everything! And he just lies in bed doing nothing… It's heart-breaking. He's completely switched off. I'm not even talking about school… forget about that.

ANNE. So you had another fight?

(**PIERRE** *buries his face in his hands.*)

Pierre…

PIERRE. I wanted so much to help him… I wanted to save him. And in the end, what's happened is the opposite… and today, we end up here… it's horrible. I so much wanted to succeed in… for things to turn out differently… to be in a better position to…

ANNE. I know.

(*She gently takes his hand as if to console him.*)

PIERRE. What are we going to do?

ANNE. I don't know. I'm as lost as you are, honestly.

(**PIERRE** *looks desperate.*)

PIERRE. Do you think it was my fault?

(*Suddenly, the* **DOCTOR** *appears.* **PIERRE** *stands up. Then* **ANNE.**)

Ah... Doctor...

DOCTOR. *(Shaking hands with* **ANNE.***)* Good afternoon. I'm Doctor Ramès. I'm looking after your son.

ANNE. Where is Nicolas?

DOCTOR. In his room. Don't worry. He's resting.

PIERRE. How is he?

DOCTOR. He's no longer in danger. You don't need to worry.

ANNE. Can we see him?

DOCTOR. He needs quiet at the moment. In the meantime, I'd like to discuss the situation with you. Sit down...

> (**PIERRE** *sits down, but* **ANNE** *stays on her feet.*)

ANNE. What's happening?

DOCTOR. The cut was not very deep, and it was treated very promptly. The worst was prevented. He was lucky.

ANNE. You're absolutely sure of that?

DOCTOR. Yes. Trust me.

ANNE. Thank God...

DOCTOR. All the same, we need to take some decisions.

> *(Brief pause. The* **DOCTOR** *gestures to* **ANNE**, *who sits down. The* **DOCTOR** *sits down himself.)*

I've been able to talk to your son... he's regained consciousness... and he seems, shall we say, annoyed to have woken up here... which is very common in this sort of case.

PIERRE. Has he said anything? About what caused him to do this?

DOCTOR. You know, we're very accustomed to these situations... and I think it would be important for Nicolas to spend a bit of time under observation.

ANNE. Under observation?

PIERRE. You mean...

DOCTOR. I've just checked and there is a vacancy in our facility.

ANNE. But how long would he need to stay?

DOCTOR. We'll decide that together. All the same, what's important is that, in this first phase, he should stay in isolation.

PIERRE. In isolation?

ANNE. What does that mean?

DOCTOR. Obviously he won't be completely on his own. There'll be the whole medical team, as well as other patients. There'll be all sorts of activities and Nicolas will be very closely supervised. But the essential thing for us is that there should be a break with the outside world. And, particularly, with the family.

ANNE. We won't be able to see him? Is that what you're...

DOCTOR. Every time we hospitalise an adolescent, this is what I ask from the parents. Systematically. It allows everyone to take some distance... to lower the stakes... to decrease the pressure... it's nothing against you, you must understand that. You don't come into it.

ANNE. But...

DOCTOR. Then, we'll meet once a week, in my office, with Nicolas, for us all to assess his progress...

PIERRE. Will this last a long time, do you think?

DOCTOR. Not necessarily. What I want is for him to acquire an awareness of what he's done. He doesn't have that at the moment. His tendency at the moment is to minimise it somewhat, which seems to me dangerous. I wouldn't want him to try it again.

ANNE. I'd like to see him, Doctor.

DOCTOR. You'll have to come back to bring him his things, obviously... But during this first week it'd be best for you to entrust him to us. Don't worry. We're familiar with these kinds of situations. Sadly, they're very common. We know what needs doing...

> *(A male **NURSE** appears. He gestures to the **DOCTOR**.)*

Excuse me a minute.

> *(He joins the **NURSE**, and they exchange a few words in a corner. **PIERRE** and **ANNE** remain silent. They're in shock. **PIERRE** takes **ANNE**'s hand. The **DOCTOR** comes back to them.)*

I'm sorry, I have to go back. I suggest you go and see my assistant on the second floor. Ask for the Department of Psychiatry.

> *(**PIERRE** is stunned by the word.)*

PIERRE. Psychiatry?

DOCTOR. Yes. She's familiar with the case. She'll give you information about what steps need taking. All right?

> *(**PIERRE** and **ANNE** don't know how to respond.)*

Come on... don't worry. He's finally in very good hands.

> *(The **DOCTOR** smiles and leaves. **PIERRE** and **ANNE** remain silent. They don't move. Pause. Blackout.)*

FOURTEEN

(**PIERRE**'s *flat.* **SOFIA** *has packed her suitcase. She's getting ready to leave for Italy with Sacha.*)

PIERRE. Are you ready?

SOFIA. Yes.

(Pause.)

PIERRE. What time is the plane?

SOFIA. I ordered a taxi. It'll be here in five minutes.

PIERRE. I'll help you down with the suitcase.

SOFIA. No, no. It's all right.

(Pause. There's a palpable tension between them.)

PIERRE. Listen, I'm sorry about last night… Sorry… I expect I'd had a bit too much to drink and… I was over the top. And stupid. I apologise.

SOFIA. I don't understand why we have to quarrel like that.

PIERRE. It's my fault. I'm sorry.

SOFIA. All we talk about is him. For weeks now… you'd think our lives entirely revolved around him…

PIERRE. I know.

(Pause.)

But it's breaking my heart to know you're going away angry with me.

SOFIA. Stop it, please.

PIERRE. What?

SOFIA. Stop saying I'm angry. That's not the problem.

(Pause.)

Why can't you come with us? Like we planned…

PIERRE. I can't, Sofia…

SOFIA. Yes, you can! The doctor told you he needs to be in isolation for a week… so what difference does it make if you're here or somewhere else?

PIERRE. I don't feel like going to the seaside, knowing he's in there. I'm sorry: I can't.

SOFIA. You could come for a few days. You need a rest as well… you're done in. It's still possible…

PIERRE. I can't. I'm sorry. I couldn't go, when… it's beyond me.

(Pause.)

SOFIA. When's he coming out?

PIERRE. Next Monday, I imagine.

SOFIA. And then?

(Brief pause.)

Why are you refusing to let him go back to his mother's? I mean, if that's what he wants…

PIERRE. I didn't say I was refusing. It's just… it won't solve the problem. And then, I don't know… after everything that happened between us… after our row… it would be such a failure…

SOFIA. For him or for you?

(*Pause.*)

PIERRE. See, the strangest thing is, I can't work out what I'm feeling any more. Sometimes it's rage and then, a moment later, it's pain. Sometimes I'm angry with him and sometimes with myself...

SOFIA. Sounds normal.

PIERRE. I hope I can be a better father to Sacha.

SOFIA. But you're a very good father, Pierre. Stop all this!

PIERRE. I'm not sure any more... what makes me sad is to have to play a part I loathe with everything in me.

(**SOFIA** *questions him with a look.*)

For example, these last weeks I keep catching myself saying things... exactly the same things my father used to say to me when I was young... things which made me genuinely loathe him... and now it's my turn. Makes me think I've finished up being just like him.

SOFIA. What kind of things?

PIERRE. "What are you going to do with your life?" or "When I was your age, I did this or I did that..." or "What are we going to do with you?" It disgusts me... I'm disappointed... in him... but in myself as well... Especially in myself. I admit it.

(*Pause.*)

SOFIA. We have to go.

PIERRE. Before you do, tell me you forgive me for yesterday. I can't let you go like this.

SOFIA. I'd really like us to stop quarrelling like that.

PIERRE. Me too.

SOFIA. These last weeks have been really...

PIERRE. I know.

SOFIA. No, you don't know. You aren't here. You're working all day, but I'm here, on my own and...

PIERRE. You're not on your own.

SOFIA. Yes, I'm on my own! And I'm tired! And there's Sacha as well. Your other son. And he needs you too!

PIERRE. Sofia, please... don't let's start again.

(Brief pause.)

SOFIA. *(More gently.)* All right. I'll call you when we get there, OK?

PIERRE. OK.

(He goes and picks up the baby from the pushchair and hugs him very tightly in his arms.)

Come on, little man... give me a cuddle... as I'm not going to see you for a week. And I'm going to miss you... Look after Mummy, will you? And your godmother as well... and you're going to discover the sea... Mm? You'll see how beautiful it is. You'll see how big it is... I'm really sorry I'm not going to be with you. But I have to stay in Paris. Do you understand? You'll tell me all about it, all right? Will you tell me about it, little man?

(He hugs him very tight. For some time. **SOFIA** *looks at him, fond and melancholy. Blackout.)*

FIFTEEN

(A few days later. The hospital. **ANNE** *and* **PIERRE** *are on their feet. The* **NURSE** *stands in front of them.)*

NURSE. Please sit down.

ANNE. How is he?

NURSE. Doctor Ramès will see you in a minute. First, I'm going to go and find Nicolas, who's close by; he wanted to talk to you before the meeting.

PIERRE. Fine.

NURSE. I'll be right back. And then I'll go and let the doctor know you've arrived.

(He goes out. **PIERRE** *and* **ANNE** *sit down.)*

PIERRE. He doesn't seem very bright, that nurse.

ANNE. Why do you say that?

PIERRE. I don't trust them at all.

(The door opens and **NICOLAS** *appears. He's in hospital clothes. He throws himself into his mother's arms and then his father's.)*

NICOLAS. Mum!

ANNE. Darling!

NICOLAS. I've missed you so much...

ANNE. We've missed you. How are you?

NICOLAS. It seems as if I haven't seen you for months...

PIERRE. We're here now. We're here...

NURSE. Nicolas, I'm going to leave you for five minutes, as you asked. To have your reunion... and while that's happening, I'm going to look for the doctor. All right?

NICOLAS. Yes.

NURSE. I'll be right back.

*(The **NURSE** leaves.)*

PIERRE. How are you?

NICOLAS. It's horrible, I swear it is. You have to get me out of here...

PIERRE. Don't worry.

NICOLAS. You absolutely have to get me out of here. Promise me?

ANNE. Has it gone badly?

NICOLAS. It was dreadful, Mum. The worst week of my life. Everyone here is sick. Anorexics, psychopaths... and... they're all crazy... they all talk about dying the whole time... I'm too sensitive for a place like this. Every night, I've been afraid... there's no lock on my door and there's this man who keeps passing to and fro in front of my room and I'm convinced he's going to come back while I'm asleep... there's another one who cries all night. All night, Mum, he doesn't stop for a single minute. I swear to you, I have to get out. You can't leave me here. It's hell. You can't leave me in hell.

PIERRE. Don't worry. That's what we're here for, to discuss it with the doctor.

NICOLAS. He's an idiot. He doesn't understand anything. He stuffs me full of pills, but he doesn't understand the first thing about what's going on in my head. He's already explained to me what he's going to tell you... He thinks I'm ill. He told me I was going to have to stay here for weeks and weeks... but I'm telling you, I can't, I won't be able to stand it... I'll crack up... You know me... you know what I'm like... I'm not saying these things just like that. I feel much worse here than I do at home... all these people, I'm finding it too disturbing. I only have one dream, to get back to normal life. And to see you. To be with you. I need you. You have to take me back home. Please, Dad, please, Mum. I'm begging you.

(**PIERRE** *is unsettled by* **NICOLAS**'s *nervous state.*)

PIERRE. Calm down, son. We'll do what's best. We'll talk to the doctor.

ANNE. Don't worry, Nicolas. We're here. We're with you.

(**NICOLAS** *smiles.*)

NICOLAS. I'm so happy to see you. I've missed you, you have no idea how much...

ANNE. We've missed you as well.

(*The* **DOCTOR** *knocks on the door and comes in, followed by the* **NURSE.**)

DOCTOR. Hello, good afternoon...

ANNE. Good afternoon, Doctor...

(*They shake hands.*)

DOCTOR. Right... I suggest you sit down. Nicolas, you can sit over here. Vincent, who's a nurse, will stay with us during our conversation.

(*Pause. The* **DOCTOR** *settles down.* **NICOLAS** *starts biting his nails.*)

Good. I expect Nicolas has communicated to you that he wishes to leave the hospital.

PIERRE. Yes.

DOCTOR. He's talked to me about it as well. I've taken it on board that, for him, this has been a testing week.

PIERRE. Yes, so it seems.

DOCTOR. Which is often the case with the first week.

NICOLAS. I don't want to stay here.

DOCTOR. I can understand that you might want to go home. But from a medical point of view, I can't allow it.

NICOLAS. *(To his parents.)* You see.

PIERRE. Why?

DOCTOR. Nicolas is going through a period of acute depression. He talks a good deal about his suicidal urges. *(To **NICOLAS**.)* You've spoken to me about it several times, remember, in the course of our conversations?

*(**NICOLAS** doesn't answer.)*

It's my opinion he'd be potentially at risk outside this institution.

NICOLAS. That's not true. I'm better. All that counts for me is to come back home. There won't be a problem. I promise.

DOCTOR. Nicolas… only two days ago, when I asked you what you'd do if we let you out today, do you remember your answer?

NICOLAS. I was trying to provoke you.

DOCTOR. I don't think so.

NICOLAS. *(To his father.)* You see… he knows better than I do what I'm feeling.

PIERRE. Calm down, Nicolas.

NICOLAS. I am calm. It's this dimwit who doesn't understand anything.

ANNE. Nicolas, please.

(Brief pause.)

PIERRE. What do you suggest?

DOCTOR. Even if this upsets Nicolas, it seems to me essential to have more time at our disposal. Suicidal impulses are sometimes difficult to identify, even for the subject himself, but we can't ignore them. They can have serious consequences, and in this kind of situation, recidivism is very common. Nicolas also suffers from a certain disconnect from reality, which causes very significant anxiety issues for him. All that can be treated. When things have been stabilised, and we find a suitable treatment, then we can think about letting him go.

PIERRE. How much time will that take?

DOCTOR. Difficult to say. Certainly several weeks…

NICOLAS. *(To his mother.)* Mum…

DOCTOR. You're safe here, Nicolas. We're looking after you. There's a whole team of doctors, nurses and teachers. And there are all our daily activities and…

NICOLAS. You think you're going to cure me with a pottery class?

DOCTOR. Yes, that's part of the process.

NICOLAS. It's a bunch of crap.

(He gets up.)

PIERRE. Nicolas! Calm down, please.

(Pause. **NICOLAS** *sits down again.)*

Do you understand what the doctor's saying? It's for your own good if…

NICOLAS. *(Interrupting him.)* For my own good? How do you think I'm going to get better if I'm surrounded by people who are much sicker than I am? I've thought about it, you know... I... all those hours of doing nothing... I've been thinking about everything that's been going on... about my life... and I'm not the same anymore... trust me... I've grown up all of a sudden. I've understood about things... things I won't do any more...

> *(***PIERRE*** looks at the* **DOCTOR**, *hoping that these assertions might have modified his position.)*

What I've understood is that I don't want to finish up in a place like this. It's been like an electric shock. And now, I feel I can return to normal life. I feel I can go back to school... I feel it. You have to trust me. It's as if I'm finally seeing the end of the tunnel. But you have to take me out of here. If you don't, I'm going under. I'm serious. I can't take it... Dad, don't abandon me... You understand me... you've always understood me... whereas they don't understand me... *(Imploringly.)* Dad... I'm begging you...

PIERRE. *(To the* **DOCTOR**.*)* What would be the procedure for taking him out?

DOCTOR. Nicolas is a minor, he's your responsibility. So it's up to you to make the decision. And in fact you could decide to take him out today. But in that case, I'd have to ask you to sign discharge papers...

ANNE. Discharge papers?

DOCTOR. Discharge papers, yes. Which will specify that you've taken this decision against medical advice. If something were to happen in the next few days, you'd be held responsible, not the hospital.

NICOLAS. But nothing's going to happen...

> *(Pause.)*

DOCTOR. I know it's a difficult decision. Especially in front of your son... but you must listen to what I'm telling you. This is not a casual opinion. Your son is in no state to leave here. You can sign these discharge papers and you'll be home in an hour... but let me tell you, as a doctor, you'll be taking a genuine risk.

> (**NICOLAS** *is getting anxious, as he senses* **PIERRE** *changing sides.*)

NICOLAS. What risk?

DOCTOR. A risk which, as a father, I would never take with my own son... Nicolas needs to be looked after and treated. That's not the parents' role. It's a psychiatrist's role.

NICOLAS. Dad... I'm not ill...

DOCTOR. If we take the right decisions, Nicolas will leave this place in good health and be able to return to a normal life. But make no mistake. The stakes couldn't be higher.

NICOLAS. Mum, I'm not ill... I want to go home...

ANNE. I know, darling... I ...

> (*She turns towards* **PIERRE**, *as if she expects him to be able to make a decision.*)

Pierre? What... I mean, I don't know... I... Say something.

> (*There's music underscoring the rest of this scene: possibly* **[ALBINONI'S ADAGIO FOR ORGAN AND STRINGS]**. *As the scene rises in intensity, the music becomes more and more present, until, in the last seconds of the scene, it's louder than the voices.*)

NICOLAS. Don't leave me here, Dad... I'm begging you... I need you...

DOCTOR. *(Trying to interrupt him.)* Now...

NICOLAS. I swear to you I understand now... you have to give me a second chance... it was a cry for help... I'm sorry about it with all my heart... I needed you to understand my pain... but I'll never do it again... I swear to you.

DOCTOR. I think your parents have heard your arguments, Nicolas.

NICOLAS. Please...

DOCTOR. *(To the parents.)* And now you're going to have to take a decision.

PIERRE. Now?

DOCTOR. Yes. It's important for Nicolas to understand that you support the medical team.

NICOLAS. Dad...

*(**PIERRE** still doesn't say anything; he's tortured by having to make this decision.)*

DOCTOR. You mustn't feel guilty. This is not about how much you love your son. It's about protecting him. In these circumstances, love is not enough. Love will not be enough.

NICOLAS. Dad...

DOCTOR. Nicolas, it's lunchtime. I'm going to ask Vincent to accompany you to the refectory.

*(The **NURSE** stands up.)*

But before that, I think it's important your parents make their decision in front of you. It will help you to accept your treatment.

NICOLAS. I want to come home... Dad...

(Brief pause.)

PIERRE. I'm sorry, Nicolas.

> *(Suddenly, **NICOLAS** jumps up, full of pain and rebelliousness, like the swelling music.)*

NICOLAS. No! Dad! You can't do that to me! Not you! Dad! Not you...

> *(The **DOCTOR** gets up, the **NURSE** tries to control **NICOLAS**. The lines may overlap.)*

DOCTOR. Nicolas! Calm down!

NURSE. Steady... Nicolas!

> *(**NICOLAS** pushes the **NURSE** away, violently.)*

NICOLAS. What have I ever done to you?

DOCTOR. Vincent will accompany you to the refectory...

> *(The **NURSE** tries to lead **NICOLAS** away, but he's struggling.)*

NICOLAS. Leave me alone! Don't touch me! What have I ever done to you?

ANNE. Pierre, do something...

PIERRE. Just a minute...

NICOLAS. Dad, help!

NURSE. Calm down.

PIERRE. Nicolas...

NURSE. Steady on...

DOCTOR. Calm down...

NICOLAS. Help!

ANNE. Pierre...

PIERRE. Stop, you're hurting him!

DOCTOR. *(Trying to intercept **PIERRE**.)* Please!

NURSE. You're going to hurt yourself.

NICOLAS. Dad! Mum!

NURSE. Come on, come with me... Please...

DOCTOR. Nicolas...

NICOLAS. Dad...

> (**ANNE** *bursts into tears.*)

DOCTOR. Come on, Nicolas... say goodbye to your parents...

NICOLAS. Dad...

NURSE. Now calm down!

> (*He leads* **NICOLAS** *away by force and makes him leave the room.* **ANNE** *is crying.* **PIERRE** *is paralysed with suffering.*)

Come on!

NICOLAS. *(Crying out.)* Dad... Dad! Dad!

> (*Pause. Blackout.*)

SIXTEEN

(**PIERRE**'s *flat.*)

ANNE. All right? How do you feel?

PIERRE. Relieved... don't you?

ANNE. I don't know. I hope we've taken the right decision.

PIERRE. I'm sure of it.

ANNE. *(Worried.)* The doctor seemed sure, as well.

PIERRE. He was saying the first thing that came into his head. And he had such an unpleasant manner. Don't you think? Do you honestly think Nicolas is ill?

ANNE. I didn't say that.

PIERRE. I prefer to trust what Nicolas told us. Don't you? He told us it was a cry for help and that he wouldn't do it again. We have to trust him. Personally, I believe him when he says this week on his own has made him understand a lot and that he's changed...

ANNE. Yes.

PIERRE. I really believe him. We have to believe him. It's important.

ANNE. You saw the way he looked when we found him in that refectory... when he understood we'd signed them, the discharge papers, did you see the way he looked? It was like seeing him again, when he was a little boy.

PIERRE. Yes. He was so happy... me too, I was as well. I couldn't have left him in there. You can't leave your child in hell... and I'm sure this will help us to start off again in the right direction. I'm sure of it. This won't all have been for nothing...

ANNE. *(Looking towards the kitchen.)* What's he doing?

PIERRE. Making tea.

ANNE. I know. But why's he taking so long...?

PIERRE. The one time he insists on doing something...

ANNE. How do you see things? I mean... down the line...

PIERRE. Seems a bit utopian to hope he'll go back to school. It's May already... If you ask me, the best thing would be for him to get strong and start again next year. After all, it's not that serious.

ANNE. But what's he going to do all day? You think you can leave him on his own?

PIERRE. I've been thinking about it and this is what I wanted to suggest to you... maybe he could come to live with you, since it seems... and during the day, I could take him to the office. To work. I mean, as an intern. What do you think?

ANNE. *(Dubiously.)* You think that would interest him?

PIERRE. In any case, he'd be looked after. He'd learn a few things. And I'd be there.

ANNE. With all the work you have on?

PIERRE. I'm going to turn down Signoret's offer.

ANNE. Are you?

PIERRE. Yes. I don't give a damn about politics or his economic programme. I want to concentrate on what really counts. And for me, what really counts is to save Nicolas. I feel it's possible now. I feel it and I don't want to let go of the feeling.

> *(At this point, the door opens and* **NICOLAS** *appears with a tray containing a teapot and cups.)*

NICOLAS. Here we are… It's ready… I even managed to find some madeleines for you, Mum.

ANNE. That's nice…

NICOLAS. You still like them?

ANNE. Yes. Unfortunately.

> (**NICOLAS** *seems to lose his balance slightly.*)

PIERRE. Careful.

NICOLAS. It's all these pills they've stuffed me full of… I get dizzy…

> (*He comes and puts the tray down in front of his parents.*)

There we are!

PIERRE. Thanks…

> (**ANNE** *notices there are only two cups.*)

ANNE. Aren't you joining us?

NICOLAS. No. I made myself a coffee. I needed to wake up. Sugar?

ANNE. No, thanks.

NICOLAS. (*Offering his father sugar.*) Dad?

PIERRE. No, thanks. Kind offer.

ANNE. All right? How are you feeling?

NICOLAS. So happy to be here. With you.

PIERRE. So are we.

ANNE. Pierre, you'll have to give me the prescription. You do have it? Then I can go and get it filled… (*To* **NICOLAS.**) I was going to go to the cinema later. Want to come?

NICOLAS. Why not? But I'd like to take a shower first. The ones in there were so dirty... I've been dreaming about having a shower all week... if it doesn't disturb you.

PIERRE. No. On the contrary...

(**ANNE** *and* **PIERRE** *laugh.*)

NICOLAS. What? Why are you laughing? I smell bad, is that it?

PIERRE. No, no.

NICOLAS. Mum? Do I smell bad?

ANNE. You really want me to answer that question?

(**NICOLAS** *watches them laughing. He looks happy.*)

NICOLAS. I like seeing you together. It's been a long time. I mean, since the three of us were all together...

ANNE. That's true.

NICOLAS. It's like the good old days...

(**NICOLAS** *smiles. Then he gets up.*)

Right. I'm off.

ANNE. See you soon. I'll wait for you.

(**NICOLAS** *takes a few steps, then turns back towards his parents.*)

NICOLAS. I just wanted to say to you... I'm really sorry about everything I've put you through just recently... I know you don't deserve it... and that it's been no joke for you. I'd like to ask you to forgive me. And above all I wanted to tell you that I love you.

PIERRE. And we love you. Come on, off you go. Don't worry. We'll be waiting for you.

(**NICOLAS** *goes out. Pause.*)

You see...

ANNE. Yes. He's back to the way he was before. Sweet and attentive...

PIERRE. Absolutely...

(Pause.)

ANNE. If you're not doing anything today, why don't you come to the cinema with us?

PIERRE. I'm not sure.

ANNE. Cheer us up a bit. And I'm sure it would make Nicolas happy...

PIERRE. I have some work to do, but... what were you planning to see?

ANNE. I need to check the times. Have you been lately?

PIERRE. No. Haven't had the time.

ANNE. Somebody told me about a film... I'm trying to remember the name... you remember the time we used to go to the cinema sometimes in the middle of the afternoon? We used to tell everyone we had important meetings, meetings which couldn't be put off, and then we'd rendezvous at that little cinema, near the Rue de l'Odéon... do you remember?

PIERRE. Of course.

ANNE. I used to love that. It felt like playing truant, didn't it? Being in the cinema while everyone else was at work...

PIERRE. Yes.

ANNE. It was so long ago.

(**PIERRE** *smiles at her.*)

Go on, come with us today! Come on... don't you want to?

> *(It looks as if **PIERRE** is about to say yes. Suddenly, there's a detonation. It's immediately recognisable as a gunshot. **ANNE** gets up abruptly. Then she rushes towards the bathroom. There seems to be a moment before what's happened penetrates **PIERRE**'s consciousness. Then, almost in slow motion, he gets up and stands motionless for a moment, frozen, as if dazed. Finally, he throws himself in the direction of the bathroom. The stage remains silent and empty for some time. Blackout.)*

SEVENTEEN

(Epilogue. Three years later. **PIERRE** *is in the living room. He seems lost in thought.* **SOFIA** *comes in.)*

SOFIA. Did you remember to buy the wine?

PIERRE. Mm? Yes, yes.

SOFIA. Great. Thanks.

PIERRE. I put it in the pantry.

SOFIA. I've almost finished the dinner. It's in the oven... I just have time to give Sacha his bath.

PIERRE. You want me to do it?

SOFIA. No, no, I'll take care of it.

(She goes over to the door and calls offstage.)

Sacha? Bathtime!

(She turns back to **PIERRE.***)*

Is it all right? Aren't you pleased they're coming for dinner?

PIERRE. Very pleased. What about you?

SOFIA. Have you noticed? Look what I found.

(She shows him the earrings.)

PIERRE. Ha!... you haven't worn them for ages.

SOFIA. Yes. I don't know. I thought they'd go with my dress.

(PIERRE smiles at her.)

Right. See you in a minute.

PIERRE. See you, darling.

(She goes out.)

SOFIA. *(Offstage.)* Sacha? Are you ready?

(Pause. PIERRE puts some music on.* Suddenly, there's a knock at the door. Is that the guests already? PIERRE checks his watch. He turns off the music and goes to open the door. It's NICOLAS.)

PIERRE. Here already?

NICOLAS. I'm not too early, am I?

PIERRE. No, no, not at all. Come in…

(They embrace.)

Are you on your own?

NICOLAS. She's on her way. She had to go and see her mother first… I expect she'll be a bit late.

PIERRE. No problem. Come in. How are you? You look well!

NICOLAS. Very good, thanks. What about you?

PIERRE. You got back this morning?

NICOLAS. Yes. It was starting to feel as if I hadn't been here for months. I was beginning to miss it.

PIERRE. How's Berlin? All going well?

---

* A licence to produce THE SON does not include a performance licence for any third-party or copyrighted music. Licensees should create an original composition or use music in the public domain. For further information, please see Music Use Note on page iii.

NICOLAS. Great. I love the city. Everything's fine. You know I've decided to move in with Élodie. Did Mum tell you?

PIERRE. Oh, really?

NICOLAS. We already spend every evening either at her place or mine… we thought it was more sensible to find a bigger place for the two of us…

PIERRE. Congratulations! That's excellent news!

NICOLAS. Yes. I'm looking forward to introducing her to you, you know.

PIERRE. And I'm looking forward to meeting her. After all this time you've been telling me about her…

NICOLAS. You'll see, she's so nice. I'm crazy about her. Have they changed the code to get into the building?

PIERRE. I don't think so, no.

NICOLAS. The code I had didn't work. Is it the same as it always was?

PIERRE. Yes.

NICOLAS. Oh, right. I must have made a mistake. How's Sacha? Is he here?

PIERRE. He's just having his bath.

NICOLAS. We got him a present. But Élodie wants to give it to him. She picked it out.

PIERRE. That's nice.

NICOLAS. And I have a present for you.

PIERRE. For me?

NICOLAS. Yes. In fact, that's why I've come early… actually, it's more something I wanted to tell you about.

(Brief pause. Then **NICOLAS** *laughs.)*

You should see your face! Don't worry! I'm not here to tell you I'm going to be a father!

PIERRE. Never crossed my mind.

NICOLAS. No, it's something more... something about me and I wanted you to be the first to know.

PIERRE. I'm listening.

(Brief pause.)

(Enthusiastic but impatient.) Well, tell me!

*(**NICOLAS** laughs again.)*

NICOLAS. You know, besides my architecture course, there was always something else I loved: writing... and recently, I've spent quite a bit of time... especially since I've been living in Berlin... I don't know why, but it all seems easier over there. It's given me some distance from all sorts of things. And helped me think about everything that was happening, when... I've always wanted to turn it into something positive. So here it is...

(He hands him a book.)

PIERRE. What's this?

NICOLAS. My first novel.

PIERRE. It isn't? You wrote this?

NICOLAS. I didn't want to tell anyone about it until I had it in my hands. Out of superstition... I was so scared... But now it's here and it really exists... I just called at my publisher's and they've given me the first copy. I wanted you to be the first person to have it.

PIERRE. *(Reading the title.) Death Can Wait.* Fantastic. When's it coming out?

NICOLAS. In two months. And if you open it, you'll see, it's dedicated to you...

> (**PIERRE** *opens it and confirms that it is in fact dedicated to him. He says nothing, but it's clear he's feeling strong emotions.*)

So, obviously, it talks a bit about what you already know... all those slightly testing years... for you and for Mum... all those difficult moments... but at least it's ended well. I wanted to dedicate it to you... because I know that, if it wasn't for you... I couldn't have...

> (**PIERRE** *takes him in his arms, preventing him from finishing the sentence.*)

PIERRE. I'm so proud of you.

> (**NICOLAS** *smiles.*)

I'm so proud. My big boy. So proud of you.

> (**PIERRE** *has tears in his eyes.*)

NICOLAS. Better wait till you've read it... you might not like it.

PIERRE. I know you. I know it'll be beautiful.

NICOLAS. Now you're not going to start crying?

PIERRE. *(Voice full of emotion.)* No, sorry. I'm just moved when I see everything you're doing... everything you've... what you've made of yourself... if we'd known when all that was going on... at the same time, I never doubted you. Never. And really, what I want to tell you is... I'm proud of you. Come on, come here.

> (*He takes him in his arms again and embraces him. After a brief pause,* **NICOLAS** *tries to disengage, but* **PIERRE** *hugs him even tighter, as if he was afraid to let him*

go. Then, they move apart. **PIERRE** *is almost embarrassed by how emotional he's become.)*

NICOLAS. Now, let's hope it's a success!

PIERRE. Of course it'll be a success… who knows, you might even become famous!

*(***PIERRE*** laughs unexpectedly. It's so gratifying, after all these years, finally to find his son has turned into this talented young man with a great future.)*

NICOLAS. Right. You don't mind if I go and give Sacha a hug? I've missed him a lot, as well.

PIERRE. Yes, he'll be happy to see you… he's always talking about his big brother.

(Strangely, instead of heading towards the back of the flat, **NICOLAS** *moves towards his old room. At the same time,* **SOFIA** *appears in the other door. She doesn't see* **NICOLAS**, *it's as if he's invisible to her.)*

SOFIA. Pierre?

(Pause.)

What are you doing?

*(***PIERRE*** is still concentrating on* **NICOLAS**, *who is about to disappear into his room. Pause.)*

Pierre? Are you talking to yourself?

(Pause. **NICOLAS** *takes one last look at him and disappears.)*

Pierre? What's the matter with you?

> (*Suddenly,* **PIERRE** *cracks and starts crying, as if he was crying for the first time. His body is shaken by a very primitive sob, his pain seems almost physical.* **SOFIA** *rushes over to him.*)

What's happening? Pierre? What's the matter?

PIERRE. (*Through his tears.*) Nothing.

SOFIA. What's the matter? Are you thinking about Nicolas?

> (**PIERRE** *nods.*)

Come on...

PIERRE. I should have paid more attention to him... I should have... I should...

SOFIA. Pierre... there was nothing more we could do. We tried everything...

PIERRE. No.

SOFIA. Yes, we did... you've nothing to blame yourself for. You did everything that was humanly possible.

> (**PIERRE** *shakes his head.*)

Come on, please.

> (*She hugs him and tries to console him physically.*)

PIERRE. (*Still weeping hot tears.*) I was trying to think about all the things he could have done... he had so much talent... he was so intelligent... and so sensitive... he could have done so many beautiful things with his life...

SOFIA. (*Trying to console him.*) Pierre...

PIERRE. *(Still weeping hot tears.)* It's all my fault... I could have done more... I should have... I should... why did I sign those discharge papers?

SOFIA. You did your best, Pierre. Believe me. Remember what the doctors told you. It was an illness...

PIERRE. No, I should have... I ...

SOFIA. Come on, calm down. I know it's hard. But life goes on. There's Sacha. And me, I'm here as well. Mm? And this evening, we have friends coming for dinner. Even if it's hard, life goes on. Life goes on, Pierre.

PIERRE. *(Descending still further into his grief.)* No, it doesn't go on! It can't go on!

SOFIA. Come on, please. Stop crying. Mm? Come here. Come to me.

> (**PIERRE** *can't stop crying.* **SOFIA** *hugs him to her even more closely, as if she was his mother. Pause.)*

Calm down, my love. Calm down... come on... shh... Everything will be all right. Mm? Calm down... you've nothing to blame yourself for. You did everything you could for him. It was his choice, Pierre. There was no helping him. And nothing you could do to stop him. Do you hear me? Nothing you could do. Come on. Calm down. Calm down, my love. And think about your little boy... he'll be four soon. Think about him. And everything will be all right. Do you understand me? Everything will be all right.

> *(She cradles him. Little by little his grief is calmed. Pause. Blackout.)*

ABOUT THE AUTHOR

Florian Zeller is a French novelist, playwright, screenwriter and filmmaker. He came to prominence with his third novel, *The Fascination of Evil*, which was awarded the prestigious Prix Interallié and nominated for the Prix Goncourt in 2004.

Between 2004 and 2020 Zeller wrote over 10 plays, including *Si tu Mourais; La Vérité* (*The Truth*); *Le Mensonge* (*The Lie*); *Le Père* (*The Father*); *Avant de s'envoler* (*The Height of the Storm*); *Une Heure de Tranquillité* (*A Bit of Peace and Quiet*); *L'envers du Décor* and *La Mère* (*The Mother*). They have been produced both in France and around the world. Since *The Truth* opened in France in 2011, it has been produced in over thirty countries, the London production being nominated for the 2017 Olivier Award for Best Comedy. His most successful play to date, *The Father*, garnered numerous awards both in France – Molière for Best Play in 2014 – and worldwide. Its London season at Wyndham's earned nominations for the Evening Standard and Olivier Best Play Awards and won Kenneth Cranham the Olivier for Best Actor. It has been produced in over 45 countries including Spain, China, Brazil, Australia, India, Israel, South Africa, Germany, Italy and Poland as well as on Broadway where it played at the Friedman Theatre starring Frank Langella (Tony award for Best Actor). *The Height of the Storm* was produced to great acclaim at Wyndham's in 2018 with Jonathan Pryce and Eileen Atkins. Directed by Jonathan Kent, it transferred to Broadway in 2019 with the same cast. *The Mother* was produced in New York at the Atlantic Theatre in 2019 starring Isabelle Huppert. Following its successful London season in 2019 *The Son* received a further 20 international productions.

All of Zeller's plays have been translated into English by Christopher Hampton.

Zeller directed his first feature film in 2019, *The Father* starring Anthony Hopkins and Olivia Colman which he co-adapted from his play with Christopher Hampton. The film was awarded two Academy Awards and two BAFTA Awards for Best Adapted Screenplay and for Best Actor. He has just completed his second film, based on his play *The Son*, starring Hugh Jackman, Laura Dern and Vanessa Kirby.

Florian Zeller's plays are represented abroad by Drama Paris / Suzanne Sarquier (www.dramaparis.com).

ABOUT THE TRANSLATOR

Christopher Hampton wrote his first play, *When Did You Last See My Mother?* at the age of eighteen. Since then, his plays have included *The Philanthropist, Savages, Tales From Hollywood, Les Liaisons Dangereuses, White Chameleon, The Talking Cure, Appomattox, All About Eve, A German Life, Visit From An Unknown Woman*. He has written the libretti for three Philip Glass operas and co-written three musicals including *Sunset Boulevard*. He has translated plays by Ibsen, Molière, von Horváth, Chekhov, Yasmina Reza (including *Art* and *God of Carnage*), Daniel Kehlmann (The *Mentor, Christmas Eve*) and Florian Zeller (*The Son, The Father, The Mother, The Truth, The Lie, The Height of the Storm* and *The Forest*). His plays, musicals and translations have so far garnered four Tony Awards, three Olivier Awards, five Evening Standard Awards and the New York Drama Critics' Circle Award.

Hampton's many screenplays include *Dangerous Liaisons, Total Eclipse, The Quiet American, Atonement, Chéri* and *A Dangerous Method*. He both wrote and directed *Carrington, The Secret Agent* and *Imagining Argentina*. His television work includes adaptations of *The History Man, Hôtel Du Lac, The Thirteenth Tale* and *The Singapore Grip*.

Prizes for his film and television work include two Oscars, three BAFTAs, a Writers' Guild of America Award, the Prix Italia, a Special Jury Award at the Cannes Film Festival, Hollywood Screenwriter of the Year, and The Collateral Award at the Venice Film Festival for Best Literary Adaptation.

**Other plays translated by CHRISTOPHER HAMPTON
published and licensed by Concord Theatricals**

A Doll's House (by Henrik Ibsen)

The Father (by Florian Zeller)

God of Carnage (by Yasmina Reza)

Hedda Gabler (by Henrik Ibsen)

Les Liasisons Dangereuses (from the novel by Choderlos de Laclos)

The Mother (by Florian Zeller)

The Son (by Florian Zeller)

Tartuffe (by Jean Baptiste Moliere)

Three Sisters (by Anton Chekhov)

The Wild Duck (by Henrik Ibsen)

**Other plays by CHRISTOPHER HAMPTON
published and licensed by Concord Theatricals**

The Philanthropist

Tales From Hollywood

The Talking Cure

Total Eclipse

Treats

Savages

**Other plays translated by CHRISTOPHER HAMPTON
licensed by Concord Theatricals**

Art (by Yasmina Reza)

Conversations After A Burial (by Yasmina Reza)

Life x 3 (by Yasmina Reza)

The Unexpected Man (by Yasmina Reza)

www.ingramcontent.com/pod-product-compliance
Ingram Content Group UK Ltd.
Pitfield, Milton Keynes, MK11 3LW, UK
UKHW021913060225
454771UK00026B/576